CONTENTS

© Bill Taylor, 2004

First published in 2004 by
Bill Taylor
Lark Rise, 47a New Street
St. Neots
Cambs. PE19 1AJ

British Library Cataloguing-in-Publication Data
A catalogue record for this book is available from the British Library

ISBN 0-9549253-0-0

Typeset in Palatino Linotype, Text by Richard Taylor in Bookman Old Style

Printed and bound in the UK by
Biddles Ltd, King's Lynn, Norfolk

Richard in Toronto
Portrait by Adrian Dingle 1938

THE RIVER GOES ON

BILL TAYLOR

© Bill Taylor, 2004

First published in 2004 by
Bill Taylor
Lark Rise, 47a New Street
St. Neots
Cambs. PE19 1AJ

British Library Cataloguing-in-Publication Data
A catalogue record for this book is available from the British Library

ISBN 0-9549253-0-0

Typeset in Palatino Linotype, Text by Richard Taylor in Bookman Old Style

Printed and bound in the UK by
Biddles Ltd, King's Lynn, Norfolk

Prologue

This book The River Goes On is the story of a family. It begins in the middle, when in the summer of 1957, having finished my initial studies at Cambridge, I was able to return to Canada. There I travelled to the place where I was born, in March 1933, on the Manitoulin Island in Lake Huron, Ontario: later I went west to Fort Pitt in the remote country of north Saskatchewan, where my parents Richard and Margaret first met, fell in love and married in 1931.

Their story is an extraordinary tale of love, devotion and a trust in the future that at times verged on the foolhardy. Richard came to Canada from the coal-mining county of Derbyshire in England following his vocation to be a priest. Margaret was the eighth of twelve children raised by Fred and Daisy Pepper, themselves of Irish and English origin. As I traced the history of Richard and Margaret's Families it was as if I was following two tributaries of one great river to their sources in two different continents.

After they were married, Richard and Margaret moved east to Ontario where, in 1933, I was born, followed by my eldest sister, Bess, in 1934. In 1938, just a year before the beginning of World War II, they moved to England, where they remained for the rest of their lives. Further children were born: Pat in 1936, who died tragically in 1990, Mary in 1939, Gillian in 1943 and John in 1949. At the time of writing, in 2004, Margaret is still alive. There are 13 grandchildren: Richard and Michael; Julia and James; Vanya, Tasha and Michelle; Edward and Peter; Stephen and Michael; Christopher and Robert. The number of great grandchildren continues to increase. It is for their sake that I have written this story because I believe passionately that it is a tale worth telling. It is a tale that gives meaning to my life; I hope it will do the same for other members of the family.

THE RIVER GOES ON

Towards the end of John Steinbeck's *The Grapes of Wrath*, when Ma and Pa Joad are contemplating their epic journey from Oklahoma to California during the dust-bowl years of the 1930s – at the same time as Richard and Margaret were trying to make a life for themselves in Canada, first in north Saskatchewan and then on the Manitoulin Island in Ontario – the following conversation takes place between them:

"'Seems like our life is over an' done'. Pa said.

'No it ain't.' Ma smiles. 'It ain't, Pa. An' that's one more thing a woman knows. I noticed that. Man, he lives in jerks – baby born an' a man dies, an' that's a jerk – gets a farm an' loses his farm. An' that's a jerk. Woman it's all one flow, like a stream, little eddies, little waterfalls, but **THE RIVER**, it **GOES** right **ON**. Woman looks at it like that. We ain't gonna die out. People is goin' on – changin' a little, maybe, but goin' right on." [1]

It is in the spirit of Pa and Ma Joad that this book is dedicated to:
Richard and Margaret,
those whom they loved
and to the memory of dear Pat.

....

---

[1] *Grapes of Wrath.* John Steinbeck (Penguin 1951) p. 388.

Foreword

A number of themes will become apparent as this story unfolds. Chief among them is the sense of undertaking a journey or pilgrimage – a voyage of exploration like that of Telemachus as he went on a quest for his father, Ulysses. The title I have chosen for this journey, 'The River Goes On', is therefore no mere whim on my part. To begin with I have paddled upstream and found the source of the river in two tributaries, one beginning in the Derbyshire coalfields, the other on the prairies of Saskatchewan. Once united in the lives of Richard and Margaret that river forms a powerful flood now spreading over the continents of Europe and North America.

On this quest it is good to have inherited from my father a deep love of history and literature. But what follows is not a straightforward piece of historical narrative. As the poet wrote: 'Time present and time past are both perhaps present in time future, and time future contained in time past'. I have therefore frequently found it necessary, as events have unfolded, to pause and look either backwards or forwards in order to make any sense of them.

Alongside this is a strong sense of 'locus' or place. Thus I have gone to a deal of trouble to set the four main geographical areas with which we shall be concerned i.e. Derbyshire, Canada - both Saskatchewan and the Manitoulin Island - and north Dorset, within their particular context, using as many historical and literary resources as I can find.

Finally, there is the sense that my own priesthood is a part of and a continuation of my father's ministry. This is best illustrated, as is so often the case, by a story:

After the Coronation Review of the Fleet, which took place at Spithead in the summer of 1953, the ships of the Royal Navy were dispatched to 'show the flag' at various ports around the British Isles. At the time I was serving as a Midshipman in HMS DIAMOND – a fine new Daring-class destroyer. On our way to Aberystwyth I was summoned to the captain's cabin. The gruff old sea-dog, Alers-Hankey, who had won a DSC in the war, greeted me with the words: "What's this, Snotty?" (a traditional title given to Midshipmen) "I gather you want to go into the Church. Are you sure it's the right thing to do?" "Yes sir", I replied, and then, without further reflection, added, "I have no choice in the matter". Those words have haunted me ever since. It was as if I was faced with an ineluctable destiny. The immediate consequence was that I left the ship for a few days to attend a residential selection conference after which I was recommended for training at university. My father in his enthusiasm sent an open telegram to the ship announcing my success. "The Midshipman's passed to be a Bish!" was flashed around the ship's company. It cost me a fortune in drinks in the wardroom.

I am proud to have followed in my father's footsteps. As the years have gone by my own sense of vocation has been fulfilled both spiritually and intellectually in many ways that he, because of a lack of education and training, could never have experienced. To have become a priest to the many descendants that he and Margaret left behind them is perhaps the greatest gift of all. It is for their sake that this book has been written.

To my own dear siblings I owe an apology. In writing a story such as this I cannot pretend to be objective. This is how I see it from my own particular perspective, as Richard and Margaret's first-born child and elder son. Many opportunities and privileges came my way which were denied other members of the family. Life isn't always fair. Perhaps I can pay a few debts by telling this tale. Because I am quite sure that it is worth telling.

Acknowledgements

A number of people and institutions have helped me in the preparation of this work - among them are: The Department of Aerial Photography in the Faculty of Archaeology and Anthropology at the University of Cambridge; Rae Benson, archivist for the Diocese of Saskatchewan at Prince Albert; Julie Bisaillon, archives technician at Laurentian University, Sudbury, Ontario, custodian of the Algoma Diocesan Archives; Katy Goodrum, senior archivist at the Cheshire Record Office, Chester, custodian of the Knutsford Ordination Test School records. Canon J. Bain Peever, the present incumbent of 'Great Spirit Island Parish' on the Manitoulin Island, made us especially welcome on our return to Mindemoya in September 2002. Cousin Ted Taylor, with his wife Evie, showed us true Canadian hospitality out at Big Lake and drove us all the way up to Elliot Lake; Uncle Bill Pepper hosted a wonderful family reunion at Lloydminster. My friend, Alistair Taylor, has given me the benefit of his wisdom over many years. Pat Chester-Kadwell has helped with the word-processing. John Wardroper has been generous with his time and typographical knowledge.

The style and contents of this finished production are entirely my own, but I owe a particular debt of gratitude to my brothers-in-law: John Newman, whose gentle prodding and encouragement kept me going and whose meticulous attention to detail has preserved me, I hope, from too many 'egregious solecisms'; Alan McMillan, whose seminal work on 'Native Peoples and Cultures of Canada' has provided a necessary corrective to my understanding of Canadian history and identity. All my siblings, each in their own particular way, have been of great help: Bess and Mary with their own memories, gracious life-styles and constant hospitality, of which Richard was (and Margaret still is) exceedingly proud; Gillian has kept me true to my Canadian roots, which become more important as the years go by. I shall never forget how she flew over the Rockies to Edmonton in September 2002 to act as a guide to our extensive 'cousinage'. John, with whom I have shared so many of my hopes and fears over the years, may now better understand where they come from: his son, my nephew Christopher, has generously helped me in exploring the mysteries of a computer. Finally, none of this would have been possible without the love and encouragement of Lottie. She has tolerated my prejudices and joined me in this exploration of my origins. Together we have returned in fact and imagination to Fort Pitt, Mindemoya and Derbyshire – she is a fellow traveller on a very special pilgrimage.

....

1 Introduction

"Go away and get your hands dirty". Walking through the streets of Cambridge in the autumn of 1956 on my way from Westcott House back to Corpus Christi College, these words rankled in my heart. Yes, I could see the justification for them. To the outward eye I must have appeared to be a somewhat naïve young man of 23, the product of my background – ten years at boarding school and a sheltered up-bringing in a remote Dorset country rectory. But I knew that I was more than that. Didn't my two years of National Service in the Royal Navy count for anything? Hadn't my experience as a sailor taught me anything about the harsher realities of life, to say nothing of keeping watch as a midshipman in a Home Fleet destroyer on an open bridge in the Arctic? But in the 1950s we did as we were told, even though the walls behind which authority barricaded itself were beginning to crack. 1956 was the year of the fiasco over Suez, which coincided with the uprising in Budapest: at home the 'angry young men' of literature and drama were asking all sorts of uncomfortable questions.

But in that autumn of 1956 I had just begun my last year at Corpus Christi College in Cambridge, where I was reading theology: if I really wanted to go forward for ordination into the Anglican ministry I needed to find a place at a theological college. In my own opinion there were only two possible contenders – Westcott House at Cambridge and Cuddesdon at Oxford. The Principal of Cuddesdon had just written an article in 'Theology' advocating celibacy, but that, I knew, was not for me. So off I went to Westcott House for a long and searching interview with Ken Carey, the Principal. I was delighted when he offered me a place at Westcott House in January 1958, thus giving me six months after the date of my graduation from Corpus to go off and 'get my hands dirty'.

The big question that remained therefore was, 'What was I to do during those six months from July to December 1957?' In the late 1950s North America was very much the promised land: many of my contemporaries at Cambridge were off to Canada and the U.S.A. It was the land of opportunities, away from a Europe still riven by echoes of the Second World War. And of all people I had an even greater reason to want to go to Canada. I was born there. My father, Richard, had travelled from Derbyshire to Canada in the winter of 1928/29 to seek ordination in the face of bitter hostility from his father, William, after whom I was named; with no other alternative he was determined to make his own future as a clergyman in the colonies. In due course he made his way to Prince Albert – a town north of the 53rd parallel in Saskatchewan, where he studied theology at Bishop's College during the winter - before moving on, in the spring, to an isolated mission based on the north Saskatchewan river at Fort Pitt. There he met my mother, Margaret (Peggy), whom he married in 1931. To pick up the threads of their extraordinary story; to try and discover what life was like in those anxious years before the war, and, perhaps in the process discover something of myself; these were the motives behind my desire to return to my roots before I entered the final stage in my own training for the ministry. That I would indeed, also, be able 'to get my hands dirty' was only an additional bonus. But, first, I had to get to Canada in the summer of 1957 and find a job to finance this journey of self-discovery.

All sorts of wild schemes were considered. With my naval experience I thought it might be possible to work my passage across the Atlantic on a banana boat, but that was quickly ruled out. Eventually, I managed both to book a return passage to Canada in the CPR liners *Empress of England/Canada* and to find a job with the Dunlop Rubber Company up at Elliot Lake in northern Ontario where deposits of uranium had recently been discovered. Internationally it was a time when the race was on to extract the ore. To find this job was an amazing piece of good fortune: a quick look at the map revealed that Elliot Lake was not far from the northern shores of Lake Huron and thus within striking distance of my birthplace on the Manitoulin Island. Faced with the prospect of this adventure, it wasn't too easy to concentrate on my final examinations at Cambridge – the delights of theology palled when compared with the excitement of exploring my roots. After a hectic round of farewell parties, I travelled to Derbyshire, where my cousin Gordon, with my grandfather William, drove me to Liverpool to embark on the Empress of Canada for Montreal.

2 Return to Canada. 1957.

The passage across the Atlantic was a liberating experience. Embarked with us were numerous emigrant families and several students, like myself, looking for adventure and new employment. Freed from an England where, not long before, food had still been rationed, some of us tried, for instance, to eat our way through the breakfast menu; this was an impossible task, as we soon discovered. I spent the whole of the long trip up the St.Lawrence River eagerly catching my first glimpse of Canada after 21 years absence. Disembarking at Montreal, I felt I was following in the footsteps of General Wolfe, who (so my father had led me to believe) trained his troops on the slopes of Hambledon Hill near Shroton for the capture of Quebec in 1759.

There followed a long overnight rail journey from Montreal to Sudbury in Ontario. Peering out of the window of my cabin in the railway sleeper at dawn it was as if I had arrived on the moon. For miles around the landscape was a scene of utter desolation. Every tree had been burnt to the ground, immense piles of sometimes still glowing slag from the nickel mines illuminated the sky. There was no temptation to linger. Quickly I caught the local train that took me further west, out into the wild and beautiful country north of Lake Huron, to Little Current on the Manitoulin Island, where I was met by my godfather, James Burt, and driven the last few miles on to my birthplace at Mindemoya.

The Manitoulin Island has now achieved some justifiable popularity as a holiday resort. The rough pre-Cambrian landscape, though of little use for agriculture, is littered with lakes and covered with trees: fine for hunting and fishing and much of the island is inhabited by native people, living in special areas or reserves. Mindemoya itself had not changed much over the years: a single main street, lined with wooden houses, in which, on the first floor of one of them, I had been born in March 1933, my cot the bottom drawer of a chest of drawers. But it was the church I wanted to see. Its construction had begun in that same year (though not consecrated until after the war, when all debts on the building had been paid off), and it was dedicated to my father's favourite saint, St. Francis. St. Francis has become a sort of icon in our family history for what may well have been one of the most fruitful periods in all Richard's ministry. In the vestry of that church I found, on the wall, a photograph of Richard, my father (and in that church, some weeks later, after I had completed my work in the uranium mines, I preached my first sermon). After a happy few days on the island getting to know my fellow Canadians, and catching an immense number of fish, in Tobacco Lake, just down the road from Mindemoya, I took off for the harsher realities of life up at Elliot Lake, some 200 miles away. On my way there I travelled up the road that had been blasted through the forests north of the trans-Canada highway at Blind River into the territory where rich deposits of uranium had been discovered not long before. The geologists and prospectors had had to fly into the wilderness in seaplanes. How transitory it all seemed when I returned again in 1994! By then all but one of the 12 uranium mines had closed down. But in 1957 all was different. In some ways it must have been like the gold rush era of the 19th century. Enormous trucks powered their way up that brand new highway through clouds of dust, the roadside verges littered with the wrecks of vehicles that had not made it. In Elliot Lake itself the first houses were being erected, though most folk still lived in trailers. Up at Stanleigh Uranium mine, my eventual destination, the labour force was billeted in long huts: it was as if we were in Stalag Luft III, or out in the Gulag, as I commented grimly to my fellow-Englishman from Cambridge and the few Canadian students who were working with us. The vast majority of the rest of the workforce consisted of homesick Portuguese men who had been imported like latter-day slaves. My most abiding memory of those days in the mines is of the melancholy 'fado' songs those men used to listen to in the evening, longing for their wives or girlfriends back at home and dreaming of the house and vineyard they would buy with all their hard-earned Canadian dollars.

But we were not slaves. Though we had to work hard, from 7 a.m. to 5 p.m, the wages were good; living conditions in the bunkhouses for someone like myself inured to anything after years at boarding school and the Navy, were almost comfortable, and the food was a revelation and, what is more, it was free – vast great steaks and, being in Canada, at frequent intervals along the mess-tables, there were pies, filled with fruits of every description, especially blueberries, which grew in profusion over the local landscape, or pumpkin. Our task, for which we were employed by the Dunlop Rubber Company, was to line great metal tanks, some 15 to 20 feet deep, with rubber sheeting. In due course these tanks would be filled with a corrosive mixture of uranium ore and sulphuric acid – the first stage in the production of the precious uranium. It was a filthy task. 'Yes, dammit', I thought, somewhat grimly, of Ken Carey, back at Westcott House, 'I am getting my hands dirty'. Standing at the bottom of the tank, painting the metal with rubber solution and almost intoxicated with the fumes. I was soon covered with the beastly stuff: the only way to survive was to think of something else – anything. As we used to say in the Navy, I thought of 'the next run ashore' – the bliss of a long shower after work and the evening meal. Sometimes there were occasional film shows, otherwise one could escape into writing letters or reading, all against the background of the melancholy fado songs. In my eagerness to get to Canada I had failed to pack many books, but a desperate message to Dorset soon produced the salvation of the Penguin paperback edition of 'War and Peace'; in my imagination, the landscape of northern Canada and Russia were fused into one.

Throughout the next 10 to 12 weeks, from mid-July to early Fall, the camp at Stanleigh was to be my home, working six, sometimes seven, days a week, with the occasional chance of a break, down on the Manitoulin Island. On one of these I took my blue-blooded friend, Andrew Kimpton, from Cambridge, to meet my fellow Canadians. Invited to share the informal hospitality of the fishing lodge belonging to my godfather down by Lake Mindemoya, we were proudly shown the only spare bedroom. In it was one large double bed. "I didn't imagine I was going to share a bed with someone else until I got married", my friend exclaimed with some disdain (after all these were the 1950s!). Somewhat nervously we shared the bed together that night. In vain next day did I try to explain that the social mores of frontier life in Canada were different from those of country houses in England – or so I imagined.

Eventually I reckoned that I had saved up enough dollars to finance the rest of the stay in Canada: my only extravagance up in the mines had been to buy a simple 35mm camera, knowing that any photographs I took would be eagerly awaited back in Dorset. But before I started the journey west to Saskatchewan I had to make another trip to the Manitoulin – to stay with my aunt, Mildred, and her husband, Dennis, whom I had discovered working up at Elliot Lake, and to preach my first sermon. I have a vivid memory of walking into Mindemoya from their simple house outside town – it only had a single water tap – down to the church on a lovely late summer evening. My cousins couldn't understand why I wanted to walk: "We'll take you there in the pick-up", they said. "Let him be", said Dennis wisely, "he needs to be on his own". I did. It was a precious moment.

....

To travel west by road from the Manitoulin Island in those days entailed a detour south-west into the United States before heading north up into the prairie provinces. The Trans-Canada Highway had not yet been completed. In any case I wanted to continue my journey by train, knowing only too well how important to the identity of Canada had been the construction of the railway lines (Canadian Pacific and Canadian National) across the continent. After all, so I had been led to believe, hadn't my grandfather, Fred Pepper, run away as a young man in 1885 to fight the Indians in their last rebellion, led by Louis Riel, against, among many other things, the construction of that railway? Even so, I was filled with a sense of retracing the footsteps of my ancestors as I journeyed west for nearly two days – from Sault Ste. Marie, up on the Algoma Central Railway to Franz in the north of Ontario, where it met the CPR line. Then on, for hour after hour sitting up in the observation lounge looking along the line of the railway, we steamed out into the immensity and loneliness of the west. I was entering 'The Great Lone Land', as William Butler described it so aptly when he travelled across this country in the 1870s. A pause for breakfast and a chance to stretch one's feet at Winnipeg before moving on to Regina (the home of the Royal Canadian Mounted Police), Saskatoon and finally the remote little town of Lloydminster on the borders of Sakatchewan and Alberta, where the kindly face of Nat Hunt (my mother's half-brother) was waiting for me at the station. With him I drove out to the north Saskatchewan river, crossing it by means of a strange antiquated ferry which was nothing more than a raft attached by pulley to an overhead wire and relying upon a rudder and the strong current to carry us over. There we arrived at Frenchman Butte – a tiny settlement by the side of the river, distinguished chiefly by two large grain elevators at the railhead. The railway itself had only been completed in 1928: it closed down sometime after the war when a bridge was built downstream over the river.

There will be a chance later to have a look at the history of that settlement on the North Bend of the Saskatchewan river, but when I arrived there in September 1957 I felt as if I had come to one of the remote boundaries of the civilised world. Frenchman Butte itself was little more than a motley collection of wooden houses scattered around the railway line and down to the river bank. There were but two trains a week – on Tuesdays and Fridays – bringing with them the mail. A simple store, built of logs, served the needs of the community: it was run by a man called Archie Wagner, who had known my parents, and he sold anything and everything, from shot-gun cartridges to flour. A little further up the hill was the church – another one-roomed structure, so small that a few years later when folk felt that it was in the wrong place they simply hitched it up behind a tractor and re-located it.

Out beyond the Butte, a few miles away, was the place I had come all that way to see – the ranch at Fort Pitt, established by my grandparents, Fred and Daisy Pepper, who had moved there in the early part of the century, before the First World War. This was the place where my mother first met my father. Sadly, I discovered that little of the ranch was left except the site on which it once stood. But not far away was the church of All Saints, the first that my father built in Canada, with its little wooden steeple dominating the porch at one end. "I built it there because Daisy Pepper wanted to see the church from the ranch", my father had told me many years earlier. He also built the church because he needed somewhere to get married. Now it is the only building remaining, and beside it are the graves of local settlers, including Fred and Daisy Pepper

The story of all this will be told later. For my own part, in 1957 I had reached my furthest point west – not until 1990 would I be able to travel on to British Columbia. Meanwhile I was content to stay in the area of Fort Pitt and the Butte, trying to catch up with the story of Richard and Margaret and, in the process, meeting all sorts of new relatives. The place was littered with them – not surprising since Daisy and Fred Pepper had 12 children. Not far from the site of the old Fort Pitt ranch was Archie Symes' spread. Another Englishman, he had married one of my mother's younger sisters, Kathleen. He was a tough character, the son of a clergyman, who had spent his way through two fortunes, yet still managed to live in a state of some confusion, with a large brood of children, my cousins, who did their best to try to tempt me on to horseback. I declined their invitation. But I was able to help Archie on the farm, driving a tractor and gathering in the harvest, even though I was not prepared to accept his offer of accommodation, in a ramshackle outbuilding that I was expected to share with one of the hired hands. Instead I decided to stay with another relative – my uncle John (one of my mother's triplet brothers) and his wife, Maud, a school-teacher, in their new house down in the centre of the Butte near the railhead. Their house boasted the luxury of central heating, located downstairs in the den, where I slept and where John kept his beer – Maud wouldn't let him bring it upstairs! John was everything an uncle should be and we took to each other immediately. "You handle a shovel quite well, for an Englishman", was an endorsement I was proud to receive from him. A poacher turned game-keeper (he was now the local equivalent of sheriff or game-warden). He was proud that I had been able to prove to him that I was no fool with a gun either. One evening a group of us, that included Archie Symes, went out duck-shooting. (It was the time of year when thousands of geese and duck were flying south over Saskatchewan on their way from the Arctic to winter feeding grounds in the United States). At first we didn't have much luck: then John and I went on ahead to lie in wait for the birds on the edge of an isolated lake, or slough, as they are called. On our way down, two ducks suddenly appeared, flying high towards me on my left. Remembering my gunnery experience in the Navy, I followed their flight, making allowance for their speed of travel, and then blasted away. To my delight the birds fell out of the air. It was a sweet experience to return at dusk, my arms laden with game, and to hear Archie mutter, "Holy cow".

2 Return to Canada. 1957.

Meanwhile winter rapidly approached over the vast and lonely landscape. There was a rush to get the harvest in. On one occasion I found myself stooking sheaves of wheat before it was brought to the thrasher, while flurries of snow blanketed the field. It was a back-breaking task and I was glad when a group of 'Indians' arrived to take over. But there was time for one more memorable trip with uncle John up the trail north to Pierceland to visit another uncle, Lloyd, and his wife Edna. Our route north took us across the watershed, over the Beaver river that drained into the Hudson Bay. On the way we passed the ruins of early homesteaders' dwellings – rudimentary timber shacks with nothing but earth sods for a roof. "In one of those", said John, as we drove past, "a lonely Swede called Gus Pedersen committed suicide. He couldn't stand the isolation. He caught the 'cabin fever'". Further on we came to Grassy Lake, where John himself used to spend months on end trapping beaver. "At times you get so used to your own company that you don't want to see anyone else: then you know it's time to get out before it's too late".

And it was time for me to get out. The river Saskatchewan was beginning to freeze over. Great blocks of ice were coming downstream and soon the ferry would have to close, thus making it impossible to cross over until the river froze solid. A final party – a sort of harvest supper made memorable by the wild laughter, fiddle playing and fun of another uncle – Harvey (one more of the triplets) – and I was on my way back to England. I can still remember vividly the moment when John drove me away from the Butte towards Lloydminster: I turned around to catch a last glimpse of that strange and haunting landscape and wondered if I would ever see it again. [I did in September 2002].

The journey home was something of an anti-climax. Having caught what must have been one of the last ferries across the north Saskatchewan river before it froze over for the winter, I made my way east. I then paused en route to stay in Regina with Henry Ellis, my father's old friend from the reserve at Onion Lake, and for another visit to Mindemoya. (It would be another 37 years before I could visit my birthplace again). Then on to Montreal, where I spent a lonely night at the Y.M.C.A., before boarding the C.P.R. liner for the voyage to Liverpool. There, I was met by the family, eager to learn of my adventures, When I finally turned up at Westcott House in January 1958 it was time to knuckle down to the rigours and austerities of seminary life.

3 Richard and the Taylors

[The repetition, throughout this chapter, of the names Richard and William, may be confusing. I shall do my best to make clear from the context to which of them I am referring: Richard I (1857 – 1882), William I – 'Daddy Doe' (1882 – 1966), Richard II – my father (1903 – 1973), William II – myself (1933 –), Richard III – my elder son (1965 -).]

During one of the summers of the late 1940s, not long after the end of the Second World War, when I was in my early teens, our father drove the family to Derbyshire for what was one of the few holiday expeditions we ever made. There were never any others, apart from rare seaside day-trips to the Dorset coast. There were just too many of us: Richard and Margaret, with the five children, myself and my four sisters, Betty, as she was called then, with Pat, Mary and Gillian, all crammed into an ancient Lanchester car. It was a journey generally made hideous because by the end of it at least one, if not all, of us was violently car-sick.

But it was always exciting to go to the old family home, St.Laurence, at North Wingfield, in Derbyshire, to stay with our grandparents, William and Elizabeth, or Daddy-Doe and Nanny, as they were called affectionately by the grandchildren. William was kind, but stern and I was aware that my father, Richard, was somewhat in awe of him. Comments would be made if we were late for breakfast, which, to my delight, always included bacon and eggs. Elizabeth was a kinder and gentler creature, presiding benignly over the extended family gathering, which frequently included our cousins, Gordon, Anne and June, from their home not far away.

One day during this visit it was arranged that my father and I should visit Parkhouse Pit, near Clay Cross, about three miles or so south of North Wingfield. It was one of a number of coalmines that surrounded the village in those days. Now every single one of those pits has been closed, but in those anxious years just after the war a desperate shortage of fuel meant that coal was mined wherever it could be found. My uncle, John Mottershaw,

Gordon's father, worked at the Holmwood Colliery, not far away. The air was filled with the smell of sulphur from the burning waste on the tips, which glowed red at night like a scene from Dante's Inferno. At the very bottom of the garden at St.Laurence, where once there was a field leading down to a brook in which we children used to play, there was an open-cast site, filled with vast machines clawing away the earth night and day.

But there was something special about the Parkhouse Pit. It seemed strange that William didn't want to come with us on our visit. It was not that he was too busy, because by then he had been retired for more than ten years. Then it was explained gently to me; "Daddy Doe doesn't want to go down Parkhouse Pit because that is where his father, Richard, was killed in an awful explosion on November 7th, 1882." As I was to discover later, this was an event which cast a shadow over the lives of both my father and grandfather in ways which only now can I begin to understand.

Conditions at the Parkhouse Colliery when we visited it in the late 1940s were primitive. There were no pit-head baths. Near the bottom of the pit shaft were stables for the ponies used to haul the wagons from the coal-face. Yet even though these ponies were only allowed on the surface once a year for a spell of fresh air and grazing, they were well loved and cared for. Crawling on our hands and knees, we made our way apprehensively ever further underground until we reached the coal-face itself. Perhaps it had been explained to them why we were there, because one of the miners took pity on me and offered me a lump of tobacco to chew. By forcing one to spit frequently it was a way of keeping some of the coal dust out of one's lungs. Gently my father warned me; "Say 'thank you'", he said, "but I don't think it's wise for you to chew tobacco at your age".

It wasn't long afterwards that the Parkhouse Colliery was closed down. Now, like so many others of those Derbyshire pits, nothing of it can be seen. But its name lingers on in the memory of that awful explosion.

Among my father's papers is a photo-copy of a document produced by W. Bassett, Printer, of Clay Cross, entitled:

3 Richard and the Taylors

In affectionate Remembrance of

The 45 men and boys who lost their lives by the

Explosion in Parkhouse Pit, near Clay Cross,

On Tuesday, November 7th, 1882.

Below this title are two columns of print: the left-hand one being 16 verses describing the disaster; the right-hand one being a list of 45 names. Among those names are two Richard Taylors, one, aged 30, from Danesmoor, the other aged 25, who was William's father, from Clay Cross. There is also a William Briggs, aged 29, from Pilsey, who was an uncle of William.

Those 16 simple verses of poetry tell a sad tale. Some of them are worth repeating:

On Tuesday morn, at ten o'clock
The people heard a deathly shock,
The news soon spread to all around
That death had worked underground.

Down number seven pit that day
Some men and boys had found their way;
The fire broke out with awful crash,
And soon their tender bones did smash.

As soon as they had felt the waft,
Some tried to get towards the shaft:
But after-damp did stop their breath,
They soon fell in the arms of death.

Exploring men went down with lights,
And soon they found some ghastly sights,
The fire burnt some, (most sad to tell),
And some in sleep had gently fell.

> *Some coffins then were quickly made,*
> *And in them the poor bodies laid,*
> *Then to the "Queen's Head" they were took*
> *For inquest and a farewell look.*

> *Poor widows thirty three are left,*
> *One hundred children are bereft,*
> *May God take care of every one*
> *Whose fathers now are dead and gone.*

The full story of William Taylor (1882 – 1966) is not part of 'The River Goes On' except insofar as it impinges upon the lives of Richard and Margaret. Towards the latter part of his life, in 1951, William wrote a simple memoir entitled **'This Is What Happened'** (TIWH), in which he describes his childhood and working life in vivid detail. Sadly he never mentions his wife's name and there are few references to his children. Of the disaster he writes:

> *My father and Uncle William worked together in what they called a stall in the pit, and as the pit was only working for about half the week, Father and Uncle William would go to the pit, along with more stallmen (when the pit was not turning or holidaying) to set timber props and make the coal face ready for turning coal the next day. There was no payment made for this kind of work, but it helped to increase the tonnage the next day, as they were paid by the ton, on the surface.*

> *It was one of those days that the explosion happened on Tuesday November 7th, 1882, at 10 in the forenoon. The village, I understand, was enveloped in a thick black smoke, with the population running towards the Colliery. It was given out later that forty-three men and three boys were in the mine, out of this number only one man survived. When the rescue men could go down the mine they found my Father and Uncle William lying by each other, their coats on, with their tea bottles in their pockets, making their way to the pit bottom. But they were overcome with gas, as they called it (Fire Damp, or After Damp). (TIWH pp. 4,5).*

3 Richard and the Taylors

Of some significance to our story is the fact that my great-grandfather, Richard Taylor, when he died, at the early age of 25, had only been married for not much more than two years. He left behind a young widow, Theresa, and two children, Florence and my grandfather, William, at that time only a few months old. William therefore never really knew his father, but he does tell us that:

> *My Father came to work for the Clay Cross Coal and Iron Company and eventually entered the pit, called the Parkhouse Pit. I think Mother told me he came from Stourbridge and was at one time a worker in some glass works. He lived at a place called Chawn Hill. (TIWH p.3)*

My own father left behind a small scrap of paper on which is written, 'Richard Taylor, son of Alexander, born 1857, probably at Chawn Hill, Hagley, Stourbridge, Worcs'. He was able to identify the Glass Works as Brierley Hill. He also left himself a note to write to the parson at Old Swinford Rectory, Stourbridge, or at Hagley Rectory nearby. He never did. But he was haunted throughout his life by the knowledge that his grandfather, after whom he was named, seems to have appeared, as it were, out of nowhere. He then married Theresa Briggs, in 1880, and lived with her for just about two years, time enough to produce two children, Florence and William, before being killed at the Parkhouse Pit in 1882. It was not until 2002 that the mystery was finally solved, when my brother-in-law, John Newman, managed to obtain from the General Register Office a copy of Richard's birth certificate. This reveals that Richard was born on the 12th October 1857 at Wallheath, Kingswinford – a suburb on the NW outskirts of Stourbridge. His parents are identified as Alexander Taylor, a coal-mine banksman, and Elizabeth, late Cadman, formerly Colley.

It would be equally difficult to trace the family line in other directions. We have a copy of the birth certificate of Theresa, who was born on November 24th, 1860, at 16 Hare Street, Bilston, Staffordshire. In this certificate her mother is identified as Ann Briggs, formerly Purcell, who married William Briggs, a coal miner, sometime during the 1850s. My father used to weave strange tales about Theresa's mother, Ann Purcell, supposing her to be the daughter of the Duke of Wellington, which I imagine are entirely fanciful. We have a copy of the wedding certificate for Richard Taylor, aged 22, and Theresa Briggs, aged 20, at the parish church of St. Lawrence in North Wingfield on February 19th 1880. We also have a copy of the wedding certificate when four years later, on June 2nd 1884, Theresa was married again, this time at Clay Cross parish church, to Elias Kirkland, aged 29. Such a marriage, if not for love, as it may well have been, was a matter of harsh necessity for a young widow, situated as Theresa was after the disaster, with two young children to care for. In his memoir William writes:

> *My Mother continued to live in Danesmoor with the small family, sister Florence, who was older than I, and myself, for some time after the explosion. She was able to earn a few shillings and there was a small income from a fund, which had arisen, called the Parkhouse Explosion Fund. Married women would receive five shillings per week and the children three shillings per week up to the age of 13 years. This money was paid out at the Clay Cross Company's offices each week. These were hard times for Mother and others. I have often thought of the scene when passing through the village. (TIWH p.6)*

They were indeed harsh times for everyone. Theresa had married Elias 'much against the family wishes'. We don't know why. Maybe they didn't want her to marry another miner. Anyway, Elias, who was illiterate at the time of the marriage, was prepared to take on the care of his two step-children, Florence and William. When they moved from Danesmoor to a place called 'The Acres' at Lower Pilsley, so that he could be nearer the colliery, he carried William, then a boy aged two and a half years old, the whole distance of two miles on his back. The house was one of a pair of four-roomed houses, with a pigsty in the garden, but it was in a 'very bad shape owing to subsidence due to coal mining and would make queer noises especially in the night'. Two years later they moved again 'to a more spacious house in High Street, Waterloo, next door to the Waterloo Hotel'. In the years that followed six more children were born to Elias and Theresa: James, Alfred, Thomas, Maud, May and John.

3 Richard and the Taylors

It was against this background that William grew to manhood. With six half-brothers and sisters, and a stepfather who sometimes used to beat him with a metal-buckled leather belt, we can perhaps understand why he became a tough character, well able to look after himself. When the time came in 1893 he was glad to leave school at the age of eleven and a half. He was the first boy from the Park House school to pass the Labour Exam. Immediately he found a job with a firm of builders and then went home to dinner, to tell the good news to his mother. Initially he had to riddle sand, but soon he was carrying bricks and mortar from 6.0 a.m. to 6.0 p.m. for a wage of five shillings a week, or about one (old) penny per hour.

On leaving school, William worked hard and conscientiously, never afraid to incur disfavour by moving from one job to another, always in the building trade, in search of better wages and prospects. He knew that he had to make his own way in the world and no one could stop him. Soon he was able to buy his own tools, which included a hammer and trowel, and when he was nearly 17 he bought his first bicycle. It cost him 13 shillings and had a fixed wheel (i.e. with no free wheel) and no brakes.

By the time he was 20, in 1902, William had married Elizabeth (Nanny). At the time, as he records in his memoir:

Work was not so plentiful, it was winter-time and I had just got married, so I took on a job with the Holmwood Colliery, to build some stables and other jobs underground. (TIWH pp. 63,64)

Very soon afterwards, on January 16th, 1903, my father, Richard, was born. On February 20th he was baptised at North Wingfield parish church.

I am now faced with the task of trying to tell the story of Richard's childhood and youth with an extraordinary paucity of evidence. While we have William's interesting and moving memoir, 'This is what happened', his son left nothing behind save a few precious documents, some faded photographs and two charming accounts of his journey to North America in the winter of 1928/29, and of his subsequent move with his young bride, my mother, Margaret, from Saskatchewan to Ontario in 1932. The rest is silence.

THE RIVER GOES ON

As 'Daddy Doe' to the grandchildren, William was a kind, if somewhat gruff figure. We know very little about Elizabeth, save that her father was called Samuel Martin, who was the foreman at the Doncaster Wagon Works in North Wingfield. She was two years older than her husband. To say that for the rest of his life Richard worshipped her and treasured her memory is not to exaggerate the depth of the relationship. He was probably a gentle, bookish character. At times he was certainly not strong physically because of a youthful attack of rheumatic fever which left him with a weak heart and which was, eventually, to lead to his relatively early death. He found in his mother the sympathy and understanding that William was unable to provide. Sometimes, when William found his son with his nose buried in a book (which was Richard's habit for the rest of his life) he would tear it from him and throw it across the room. Later, when Richard was homesick and lonely in the emptiness of north Saskatchewan, it was his mother who kept him supplied with precious boxes of books. In my own library I possess a volume, given to me by Richard at Easter 1956. It is called 'The Thousand Best Poems in the World'. It carries this inscription: 'This book of poems belonged to my old schoolmaster, James Hoddes, of North Wingfield, Derbyshire. He was also my father's old master. He sent this volume to me in Canada in 1928 and I had it rebound in 1947'. It is therefore no surprise that each one of his own six children, in addition to the sometimes curious additional names (William de Carteret, Elizabeth St. Denys, Gillian St. Francis) also carry his mother's surname – Martin. When, to our great delight, my young brother was born in 1949, Richard asked me to be his godfather. I naturally agreed, but on one condition, "You don't lumber him with so many Christian names. Just two will be sufficient – John Martin".

On June 23rd 1904, Richard's sister, Dena, was born. She was to marry John Mottershaw, in April 1929, while Richard was in Canada. She remained in Derbyshire for the whole of her long life, fiercely loyal to the family connections with North Wingfield. Mottershaws have lived there for centuries. To this day, Gordon lives but a few yards from the old family home of St. Laurence, with his own son, Michael and family, just next door.

Richard's only brother, Alexander (Alec) was born in 1906. In 1936 he moved away from the village with his wife, Vera, after what must have been a monumental row with his father William. Apparently, like Richard, he refused to work with his father in the family building business. It may have been more than that because all further relationships with the rest of the family were severed and his name was rarely mentioned. Only when I travelled to North Wingfield to officiate at William's funeral in 1966 (Richard being ill in hospital at the time) did I meet Alec my uncle for the one and only time in my life.

About the time of Alec's birth, William moved with the family to the village of Rusper near Horsham in Sussex. He tells us that Elizabeth had an uncle, Minall, who worked as a builder and decorator there with his son-in-law, Oakley. It had been suggested that William might like to join the firm. This he did for a while, just four months, then he left, as he recorded somewhat cryptically in his memoir, 'for various reasons'. William always liked to be his own 'gaffer'. His next job was 'estate man' for the nearby Courage family at "The Mount" and there he remained until the family returned to Derbyshire in 1911. One of the few precious early photographs we have of Richard is taken at this time. In it, at the age of 8, he is dressed in formal knickerbockers, with an Eton collar, leaning on a fence and looking wistfully at the camera, while, to the right, is the stern figure of his father, William, talking, not to his son but to a huge dog. But of the school that Richard must have attended at that time there is no record.

This silence about Richard's education is one of the mysteries of his childhood and youth. Another early photograph, taken soon after the return to North Wingfield, shows him in the boys' school there. It is a formal scene, the boys sitting rigidly to attention, their hands behind their back. In it Richard can just be identified – a boy wearing glasses, third from the right in the back row. It may also be possible to identify him in a large group of Church Army or Crusader lads and lasses, sitting shyly to the front and left of the leader. Perhaps this is a photograph of the local branch of the 'Church of England Temperance Society', because in April 1914 Richard was issued with a Certificate of Merit, First Class, for 'Proficiency in Temperance Knowledge' (The Religious

Aspect). But the best photograph we possess is another one taken of the three children a little later: Dena, with her brothers, Alec and Richard, who was then sporting a waistcoat and watch chain.

But there is no record of Richard's schooling, and nor did he ever talk about it with his children in later years. It is almost as if he wanted to draw a veil over the whole process. One can guess that with his love of books and reading and his lack of much physical vigour, he did not relish the rough hurly-burly of William's building-yard, much to his father's disgust. We can therefore only conclude that he left school at 14, towards the end of the First World War, from which his father was exempt, being, for some reason, 'not fit for any Military Service whatever'. Instead William 'was drafted to buildings of urgent necessity, for works on railways and collieries'. (TIWH p. 70)

At some stage in his youth Richard must have been drawn more closely into the life of the Anglican Church. William had not remained loyal to the Methodism of his mother, Theresa. Richard was baptised in infancy at the parish church of North Wingfield. In some notes for a sermon that he preached at Shroton towards the end of his life, Richard refers with real affection to the influence of the kindly rector: "I grew up as a boy in a Derbyshire mining village. The new rector was Arthur Ellerton. As a very young choirboy I was asked to be a server. On and on there were some wonderful services as the years went by under the patient Rector. And so I was taught to venerate the sacred mysteries of the Church". In 1924, at the age of 21, we know that Richard also had a brief flirtation with the idea of politics. During that year he was the agent for the Conservative party in East Bradford and we have a photograph of him, clad in white tie and tails, at the Conservative Ball held in January. By that time he had certainly moved away from home, Cross Cottage, in the centre of North Wingfield, because on one of the few occasions when William refers to his family in his memoir he wrote:

On looking through the windows of Cross Cottage you could plainly
see the house opposite – St.Laurence. (It used to be the curate's
residence). One day my son, Richard, who was at home for a short
period and I were looking through onto 'St. Laurence' and he suggested

it would be nice to buy it and live there. "Yes", I said, "your Mother and I thought that so we purchased it about 4 or 5 months ago". He was very pleased for he shouted out "Hurray". (TIWH pp. 73,74)

It is good to note this moment of happiness between father and son because I suspect that there were not too many during those uncertain years of the 1920s. Richard had left school; like his brother Alec he had no desire or aptitude for the building trade; a life in politics was never a viable option, because an agent was paid almost nothing, nor was there any possibility of going to a university. For someone of his background and education it was quite out of the question at that time. What therefore should he do? Maybe the idea of ordination came into his mind from the kindly Rector, Arthur Ellerton, who, as we have seen, took an interest in this gentle lad from a rough Derbyshire mining village. In 1924 Richard went to learn something of the nature of parochial ministry by staying with clergymen. He went first to stay at Tean Vicarage in Staffordshire with the Revd. F.H. Alexander, then to Maltby Vicarage in Yorkshire with the Revd. H.R.Everson. There is evidence, from an inscription on the flyleaf of one of his precious early books, that during February and March 1926, he was living at Spring House, Heckmondwike, in Yorkshire. There is evidence that in September 1927 Richard went for training to the Knutsford Test School at Hawarden near Chester. [I discovered this in the summer of 2003 when investigating the records of the Knutsford Test School now held in the Cheshire Record Office at Chester]. The Test School was an extraordinary venture founded by 'Tubby' Clayton of Toc H [see note at the end of this chapter] after the First World War for young men, inspired or driven by the horrors of trench warfare, who wished to go forward for ordination but were unable to do so because of a lack of formal education. It started initially in December 1918 at the Old Machine Gun School in Le Touquet with 170 men and it then transferred in March 1919 to Knutsford Gaol in Cheshire, that being the only accommodation available. Prison cells were turned into studies and the corridors into a dining room or recreation space. In 1921 'civilian' students were welcomed and in January 1925 it transferred to The Old Rectory at Hawarden in

North Wales, near Hawarden Castle, the residence of the Gladstone family. A basic syllabus in Latin, Greek, History and Maths was offered, sufficient to qualify the ablest students for entry to college or university. Richard's record card states that he was sponsored by the Diocese of Bradford to the tune of £60, a further sum of £55 towards the total fee for the year of £115 being paid presumably by his father. The magazine of the Test School for Michaelmas 1927 (Volume V, number 1) was edited by Richard and under 'Toc H notes' it records: 'At the beginning of the term we welcomed the following members who came from their respective branches to commence their training at the school – R. Martin Taylor of Spen Valley, Yorkshire, and Chesterfield'. The records do not tell us much about the rest of his time at Hawarden, nor was there any real chance for him of going to university in England.

Then, suddenly, a solution appeared from an unlikely source. It might be possible to get ordained by going to work abroad. The "colonies" – in this case 'The Church of England in Canada' - were then regarded as the missionary territory of the church. The need for missionaries was great, the academic qualifications demanded were not so stringent, and the cost was not so prohibitive. Perhaps the Bishop of Saskatchewan, the heroic George Exton Lloyd, or one of his commissaries appointed for that purpose, had visited England on a preaching and recruiting mission, calling young men of vision and courage to work in the young colony. We do not know the details, but something of this nature must have happened, providing Richard with a solution to his problem. No doubt with much opposition from his father and quiet support in the background from his mother, Richard responded to an urgent invitation from Bishop Lloyd to come to Canada for training. Somehow or other William was persuaded to part with £74. 13s. 8d – 'on account of passage money etc, in connection with Mr R.M. Taylor's journey to Prince Albert, Saskatchewan'. The receipt is dated December 15th, 1928. Richard was then just one month short of his 26th birthday.

....

Richard with his father, William, in 1910

Richard, Alec and Dena

W. A. Taylor, Daddy Doe [The Gaffer] with the sanitary inspector

Richard circa 1924

Peppers at Edam, Saskatchewan 1912
Daisy with Peggy, Grace, Rose, Nat, Fred
Triplets (Charlie, Harvey, John), Lloyd

Peggy and Dinah at Edam, circa 1913

Fred Pepper with his Pigs at Fort Pitt

Peggy at Fort Pitt 1930

Peggy on the Puddle Jumper

Wedding day 17th August 1931

Fort Pitt Church (circa 1970)

Richard and Margaret at Mindemoya 1932

Margaret

Laying the foundation stone of St. Francis Church
15th June 1933

St. Francis Church
December 1934

TOC H

Talbot House, or 'Toc H' at it came to be called, was founded in 1915 during the First World War, when a large house at Poperinge in Belgium, just behind the Ypres salient, was acquired for use as a soldiers' club. It was named Talbot House in memory of Lieutenant Talbot who was killed in 1915: his brother was an army chaplain and their father was Bishop Talbot of Winchester. Toc H comes from the army signallers' code for 'T'. The inspired chaplain who ran Toc H was the Revd. Philip 'Tubby' Clayton, who like others in the First World War such as Dick Sheppard and Studdert-Kennedy ('Woodbine-Willie') had a wonderful talent for friendship and pastoral care. A notice hung by the front door of Talbot House bore the message "All rank abandon, ye who enter here". Tubby Clayton kept a card index of young men who had expressed a wish to go forward for ordination when the war was over. Out of this arose the Knutsford Test School.

After the First War Toc H quickly expanded throughout the English-speaking world. Residential hostels were founded in many major cities where young men could find a home and friendship while seeking work. The symbolic lighting of a Toc H lamp became a link with the original house at Poperinge, which still stands. Toc H at Toronto was Richard's base while he worked for the Algoma Diocesan Endowment Campaign. Tubby Clayton lived to a great old age in London. I met him once in 1955 (or thereabouts) when Toc H was helping me towards the cost of my ordination training.

4 A Journey West

[Sometime during the 1950s Richard was persuaded to write an account of his work in Canada. Many tales had been told to us children about those early days, but there was no definitive record. In due course he produced just two chapters, the manuscripts of which have survived among his papers. The first describes the initial Journey West to Canada in the winter of 1928/1929: the second describes the move to the Manitoulin Island in 1932 and the construction there of St. Francis' Church. I have reproduced these two chapters without any attempt to alter their style or content because they seem to reflect the enthusiasm, optimism, naivety and courage that enabled Richard with Margaret to survive numerous adventures and misfortunes.]

....

A cable from that grand old Bishop of Saskatchewan, the Right Revd. George Exton Lloyd, really began things. **"DEFINITELY ACCEPT YOU FOR SASKATCHEWAN. ARRIVE PRINCE ALBERT JANUARY 1ST 1929".**

I embarked on the RMS *Majestic* at Southampton on December 18th, the good Bishop having given me ten days to announce my decision to go abroad to my parents and friends; to pack up all my belongings and to make my farewells. I must confess that it was not until I had seen the shores of the Isle of Wight fading in the dim haze of the early morning that I began to wonder what kind of adventure this was going to be.

It was the week before Christmas and life aboard the *Majestic* was a very jolly one for most people; crowds of returning Americans and Canadians going back to their homes for Christmas. I was travelling Tourist and although I was not in orders, being just a humble theological student, the purser asked me if I would be responsible for divine services on the ship and so I was given the freedom of the boat and thus able to meet many people as we got out into the Atlantic Ocean.

The first two days were lonely enough for me, goodness only knows, and the ice was first broken at the dining-table. My companions were a married couple from

Cuba, Father Kiaran O'Duffy, a young Franciscan monk going out to St.Elizabeth's Seminary in Denver, Colorado; and a young French-Canadian lady.

Father O'Duffy was a fine young Irishman about my own age and we became quite friendly. He confessed to me that he, too, shared my feelings of loneliness. We swapped cigarettes and had many talks in each other's cabins. He had said "Good-bye" to his old parents in Ireland. The tears came into his eyes as he told me that it was improbable that he would ever see them again. I think that in our many promenades around the decks we learned a great deal about each other's communions and perhaps because of Father O'Duffy I have never since been able to share in the extreme protestant hatred of the Church of Rome.

On the third day out I noticed a very tall man of striking appearance enveloped in a long coon-skin fur coat. I seemed to be continually bumping into him and meeting his very keen scrutiny. It was not long after he stopped me as I was going up into the library, held out his hand and said; "My name is Windham, Sir Walter Windham. I have been watching you a good deal and I like the look of you. What is your name and where are you going?" I told him that I was an ordinand going out to do missionary work in the Diocese of Saskatchewan. He said, "Fine! There are some people on the boat I want you to meet. You come along with me." He took my arm in a vice-like grip and piloted me to a corner of the lounge where four men were discovered sitting around a table and proceeded to introduce me to them. They were introduced to me as Dr. Frank Buchman, Mr. Graham Brown and Mr. Van Lennep. I fail to recall the name of the fourth man. These men were dressed in lay attire and I was not able to find out until much later that the man introduced to me as Mr Graham Brown was a priest of the Church of England. (He is now Anglican Bishop in Jerusalem). The other young man, whose name still escapes me, was also an Anglican priest from Oxford. Dr. Frank Buchman is, of course, still the guiding spirit of the Oxford Movement.[2] I think Mr. Van Lennep was a South African.

The following Sunday I was responsible for four services on the ship and, having prepared a special

---

[2] In 1938 this became known as 'The Moral Rearmament Movement'. It has been condemned latterly for its disingenuous use of the name Oxford for its methods of enforcing 'conversions' on unsuspecting individuals. It is a relief that Richard managed to escape from the clutches of this organisation.

Christmas sermon, delivered it at four times in different parts of the ship. Sir Walter Windham and my new acquaintances attended every service with me and very bravely listened to the same very amateurish effort each time. Imagine my horror when later I discovered that, due to heavy seas and the slow crossing we had made, we should not reach the harbour at New York until Christmas Day. Plans were made for a midnight service on Christmas Eve. Mr Graham Brown, now known as a priest of the Church, celebrated the Holy Communion, assisted by the other young priest. On the other side of a partition in the main lounge, Father O'Duffy said Mass for his flock. After the services we met in the purser's cabin for a glass of wine, a smoke and a long talk.

Soon after our first meeting, Sir Walter and his party invited me to a little gathering which met each morning in one or other of their cabins, or on the deck aft, following breakfast. Accepting the invitation, I found my new friends armed with Bibles; Dr. Buchman read a portion of Scripture and then suggested that we should have a "quiet time and wait for the guidance of the Holy Spirit." We kept silence which was only broken when Dr. Buchman said "the Holy Spirit tells me that Taylor should join our house-party in New York." I asked, "What house-party is this?" It was explained to me that the group was crossing from England and proceeding to some hotel in New York where they were to meet people and have a sort of convention to discuss things of the Spirit. I said, "I am very sorry but I am going to stay with my aunt and uncle in New York; I haven't seen them for many years and as I have to be in the far West on the first of January I am afraid that I shall not have the time to come to your party." And there the matter rested until the meeting the following morning, when Dr. Buchman again brought up the question of my going to the house-party in the New York hotel. He suggested that we should have a further "quiet time" in order to get fresh guidance from the Holy Spirit on this question. We closed our eyes and bowed our heads. The silence was rudely broken by Sir Walter, who suddenly exclaimed, "Now that is not fair, Frank. You haven't got your eyes closed and you are writing in your note-book!" Dr. Buchman replied, "when the Holy Spirit gives me guidance I must write it down. I am quite convinced that it is Taylor's duty to obey the Holy Spirit and come to our house-party!" Sir Walter retorted, "I am an old naval commander and if I tell my men to do something I expect them to do it. If Taylor's bishop has told him that he must be in Saskatchewan on the first of January, well, there he must go." And so the matter was settled once and for all and I did not go to the house-party.

Christmas morning was a cold and damp one. We were on deck very early to get our first glimpse of the famous Statue of Liberty. We indulged in a little good-natured chaffing with our American friends and heard something of the old jest about the back of the figure of Liberty being turned upon the "brave new world."

Then the marvellous skyline of New York's skyscrapers hove into view; the huge buildings piercing the blanket of mist like the teeth of some enormous dragon. We were approaching one of the world's busiest harbours. It seemed to me a miracle that we did not collide with the hundreds of tug-boats and ferries which covered the surface of the water. Slowly the huge bulk of the *Majestic* was manoeuvred alongside the dock and then, what a rush and commotion - the business of passports and customs and what appeared to be a veritable bedlam of confusion! We were obliged to pass the scrutiny and questioning of the immigration officials as they sat at a desk in the main lounge. Grouped under the initial 'T', I almost brought up the rear of the long serpentine queue which stretched from the desk in the lounge and along the gangways outside. It seemed as though I would be hours before I reached the officials. Sir Walter Windham was quite at home, walking about with a comfortable cigar in his mouth. Presently he espied me near the end of the procession of supplicants. He said, "What are you doing here, Taylor? I have been hunting high and low for you. I'm going to see you safely off the ship. You come along with me." I meekly followed his huge bulk to the desk of the immigration officials in the lounge. Arriving there, he perched himself on the desk, much to the official's annoyance. "Who are you?" the man asked. "I am Windham. Sir Walter Windham." "Oh yes, Sir Walter. And what can we do for you today?" "I want you to have a look at this man's passport, for he is leaving the ship with me." In a matter of seconds my passport was stamped and we were making our way down the gangway. Sir Walter guided me to the 'T' section in the great shed on the dock and we said "Goodbye" and shook hands. The customs officials near the huge piles of luggage looked a little cross – probably because they had been kept away from their Christmas dinners due to the late arrival of the ship. In trying to unlock one of my cases for inspection the wretched key jammed in the lock and remained immovable. The officer said, "Never mind about that one; let's have a look at another one." The moment our backs were turned a negro customs assistant came along with a steel crowbar and pried open the offending lock before we noticed what was happening, ruining my nice new leather case in the process. I was about to give suitable expression to my feelings when I heard a feminine voice calling "Richard!" I turned towards the voice and discovered my aunt, whom I had not seen for many years, standing by the barrier. I rushed over to greet her. When I returned to collect my luggage I found that it had been cleared and all was well. My uncle was awaiting us out in the street at the wheel of his car. We drove through New York down to the Lackawanna ferry and crossed over to their home on the other side in New Jersey.

I spent a wonderful time with my aunt and uncle and cousins. I was hurled around from one place to another. I saw so many things; lived in such a state of hurry and bustle for the next few days, that my impressions of that stay are very confused and blurred. I did achieve an ambition, cherished from boyhood, when I persuaded my uncle (to his secret disgust) to take me to the top of the Woolworth Building, then the highest on Manhattan Island. I wish I could recapture the thrill I experienced as I gazed down upon the human insects crawling about the streets far below. My uncle stood with his back to the wall of the centre tower protecting himself from the icy wind, puffing his inevitable cigar, and regarding me with a look of mingled pity and tolerance.

But the time to leave came all too quickly. On the morning of the 27th I was driven to the Grand Central Station, a clean, imposing, smoke-free terminus, and the second stage of my long journey was begun.

The train reached Montreal at nine o'clock that evening. Montreal! The gateway to Canada! A city that is probably more French than Paris itself. A city of great wealth and great poverty. A city of fine churches and foul slums, as I was to discover in later years.

At ten o'clock that evening, the long journey to western Canada began and I experienced my first night in a communal sleeping-car. When one has discovered how to undress in a space as large as a good-sized coffin, the main difficulties have been mastered, and one can rest very comfortably between scrupulously clean sheets. The coloured attendants are most obliging and courteous, and materially help to smooth out the difficulties which arise when twenty people live and sleep for the better part of a week in a compartment the size of the entrance hall of a suburban home.

Next morning I was awake quite early. I looked out of my window to see a world white with snow, very beautiful and very grand, rushing past. Unbuttoning the brown canvas curtains on the other side of my bunk, I peered cautiously out into the gangway between the rows of sleeping berths. A symphony of snores from a dozen healthy sleepers assured me that it would be safe to venture to the mens' dressing-room. There I found a coloured attendant assiduously polishing the row of four chromium-plated washbasins. He greeted me with a "Good morning, sah!" and we entered into a most interesting conversation as I shaved. "So you's a preacher, sah!" he said. Dreadful memories of my Christmas effort on the *Majestic* rushed to me, and I replied, "No, I'm afraid not. I'm just going to be a missionary". "No, sah", he retorted, wagging a forefinger at me. "Ah know you's a preacher. Ah comes from Alabama. Ah ain't a-goin' to be on de railroad all ma life. Ah's savin' ma' money. Ah's gwin to be a mortician". "A what?" I exclaimed. "You don't know what a mortician is?" he asked incredulously. "A mortician is de man as lays out de corpse and puts it in de casket. A mighty fine payin' job is de mortician. Ah always makes friends wid de preachers, fow we has to woike together". I hope that my coloured friend has now reached the summit of his ambition. I like to picture him now as a prosperous undertaker somewhere in sunny Alabama.

I remember, with much pleasure, those four very interesting days spent on the trans-Canada railway. I became very friendly with a tall sheep-farmer, who was returning, via Vancouver, to Australia. His intense loyalty to the Crown and his deep reverence for the Old Land (which he had just been visiting for the first time) much impressed me. We spent many happy hours together in the observation coach. I well remember one incident. The official in charge of that coach was a very surly individual who performed his duties with an air of condescension and martyrdom. I remember him as a man with a very jaundiced outlook upon life, as one born to suffer and be oppressed. One afternoon, my Australian acquaintance was speaking about the Royal family to me. He said that he thought the Prince of Wales was a "mighty-fine chap!" The remark was overheard by the attendant at the other end of the coach, for he came up to us and said to the Australian, "Bah! Royalty are just parasites. We have to pay to keep the likes of them in luxury. If the King were to come on this train I would take no more notice of him than I would of a fly." I did not like the look of the grinding motion of the lower jaw of my Australian friend as the champion of democracy unburdened his tortured soul. It was like sitting on the edge of a smouldering crater. The man from the Antipodes slowly rose from his seat and drew himself to his full six feet four inches and glared down upon the hapless man as one would upon a loathsome reptile. He seized his shoulder, held in a vice-like grip and said in a slow, drawling voice, "Say guy, I guess you'll take back every word you've said or I shall be obliged to push them back one by one down your dirty throat!" The attendant, by this time thoroughly scared, suddenly remembered some matters of importance at the other end of the train requiring his immediate attention and beat a hasty retreat.

We did not see him again until the evening, when he came into the pullman where we were sitting. Approaching us he said, "I hope you gentlemen will forget what I said this morning. I don't want to lose my job." The lecture he then perforce had to listen to from the representative of the Australian Commonwealth was terse, brief, but very much to the point. It was calculated to recall, to a fresh and higher sense of duty, one who was at once an employee of a great Canadian railway and a subject of His Imperial Majesty. Fortified with these words of wisdom and happy in the knowledge that his untimely outburst would not "go any further", our observation-car conductor was a changed man from that moment. His attitude from that hour was that of a man who has seen a great light and is determined to walk softly for the rest of his days.

The greater part of the journey across Canada is through much wild and uninhabited country. One travels for miles and miles through snow-covered wastes and into the heart of what must have been a tremendous forest. Here great fires had consumed much of the virgin timber and had left thousands of melancholy charred stumps. Occasionally the train would pull up to take in fresh water for the engine, fresh supplies of food for the dining-car and the tanks of ice-water for the use of passengers would be refilled. We were always glad of the opportunity to get down off the train to stretch our legs and perhaps exchange a greeting with some trapper or settler who had journeyed down from the north to collect supplies. Or perhaps there would be a Hudson's Bay factor who had come to start off a shipment of raw furs on their journey to London, the centre of the world's fur markets.

Then the conductor would shout, "All aboard!" and away we would go. As we pulled away from each depot there would be a few log cabins near the edge of the railway track where we could see the wives and children of the trackmen standing at the doors and waving "goodbye" to the train, which had brought its daily bit of excitement and interest into their lonely lives.

The temperature was well below zero. One could appreciate the practical value of the triple glass windows in the coaches. And so to Winnipeg, which was reached at ten o'clock on Sunday night. We took advantage of a halt at the station and some of us decided to see what we could of this Western City of the plains. The temperature that night was 45 degrees below zero, so we were told, and the wind, which blew along Winnipeg's tremendously wide streets served to intensify the acute cold. Some of us felt that a cup of hot coffee would be a good idea and a kindly Irish policeman directed us to a drug store. It was a new experience to be perched on a high stool at a counter in a pharmacist's shop drinking coffee on a Sunday evening, but I soon discovered that one could purchase almost anything at any time of the day or night in the drug stores on this side of the world. Very useful institutions they are, usually very clean and spotless and manned with obliging staff. After our return to the station we were glad to get back to our super-heated pullman. Through the night, to the mournful accompaniment of the engine's siren, we sped across the prairie to the city of Saskatoon.

Saskatoon is a modern city with wide streets and fine buildings. Some twenty-five years before it had been a town of tents and shacks. Here the Barr Colonists from England and Northern Ireland had landed and stayed for a few days until their trek up north was organized.

Then the last stretch of the journey, the two hundred miles due north to Prince Albert. As we travelled north we left the prairie behind and entered rolling bush country. I reached Prince Albert just before midnight on the 31st December 1928 and had travelled over 6000 miles and arrived punctually at my destination. I was met on the platform by some of the men from Bishop's College, headed by that fine priest, Canon Strong, then Rector of Prince Albert and the pro-Cathedral and a lecturer at the college. We checked my baggage at the station and then they took me down into the city, where we invaded a Greek restaurant and consumed large quantities of roast turkey and green-apple pie, washed down with pints of delicious coffee. Prince Albert looked like a fairy city, with brilliantly lit streets, and sparkling snow at the edge of the side-walks. In front of many of the stores and in the gardens of the houses were Christmas trees, illuminated with many coloured electric bulbs. The city at night, its straight streets stretching up from the broad north Saskatchewan river, the jingle of bells, the thick furs of the pedestrians, made me think irresistibly of all I had read of Moscow, the Tsars, Tolstoy, Turgenev, Tchekov, and the host of them.

I found the college to be a pleasant building on the hill overlooking the city. It had been conceived and planned by the Bishop of Saskatchewan, George Exton Lloyd[3] to fill a definite need in view of the tremendous development of Saskatchewan and the influx of thousands of emigrants from the British Isles and different parts. He needed a large band of missionaries to go and work amongst these people. The numbers of ordained volunteers from England and eastern Canada were not adequate to meet the pressing need for men to open up the pioneer districts and so, as he had done at Saskatoon years before, he established a college in the city of Prince Albert for the purpose of training men for missionary work in his own diocese. The training was very intensive; sometimes very hard, for the men had to cram a year's work into the weeks between Christmas and Easter. For the rest of the year they went out to their work in new missions. The bishop had gathered around him an excellent body of lecturers, and here I must mention Archdeacon W.E.J. Paul, Archdeacon to the Indians, who exposed us to some New Testament Greek. A real saint of God, this priest – he and his wife have laboured faithfully and unheralded for many years amongst the Indian missions of that part of the great

---

[3] Bishop Lloyd, when he was still a theological student from Toronto, volunteered to fight Indians and was wounded during the Riel rebellion in 1885.

province of Saskatchewan. Other lecturers were Canon Burd (who succeeded Bishop Lloyd as Bishop of the northern portion of the Diocese of Saskatchewan, when it was afterwards divided), Canon Stevens, Canon Holmes, and the good Bishop himself. The bishop's lectures were the most interesting of them all, for with very little persuasion the subject of his lecture would go by the board and he would treat us to many interesting stories and reminiscences of the pioneer days in the West. Probably his accounts were of more permanent value than Dogmatic Theology and the other subjects about which he was supposed to be lecturing. It was a surprising thing for me to find that practically all the men in the College were from the British Isles, for at this time I seem to remember that Canon Strong was the only Canadian-born amongst us. I found this to be true all over the diocese. The missionary work was in the hands of men from the Old Land. Bishop Lloyd is a great Imperialist, and had grand ideas about 'making Canada British'. The good bishop thought that it was a huge mistake that emigrants from central Europe should outnumber those coming from Great Britain to settle in the West.

Prince Albert is a very 'English' city and I met very many charming people from the Old Land who opened their homes to Bishop's College men and certainly helped to make our sojourn in the city a very pleasant one. These kind folk kept open house for us and brewed many thousands of cups of tea.

The city is the 'Gateway to the North'. Here the great trading companies have their headquarters and amongst them is the Hudson's Bay Company. I was there in time to see the great change which was taking place. For many years all the supplies had to be taken up to the north country by dog teams, but aeroplanes were coming into their own, and what used to be a journey of from six weeks to two months was now accomplished in a few hours by air. In winter these machines, equipped with skis, land on the ice of the frozen north Saskatchewan River. The climate in winter is most exhilarating and if one is well wrapped up in furs, and the journey not too long, the cold does not occasion any great discomfort. This is probably due to the extreme dryness of the air, although it was very necessary continually to rub one's nose, cheeks and forehead, to make sure they were not being frozen. It is no uncommon thing, when out of doors in the winter, to meet a complete stranger, who will proceed to rub one's nose and face with a handful of cold, dry snow and explain the action afterwards. When the extremities begin to freeze, the owner of them is not conscious of what is taking place, but the friendly passer-by perceives the whiteness of the exposed parts of the face and realises that they are being frozen; a prompt rubbing with a handful of snow is the sovereign remedy.

In this delightful and busy fashion the end of the term drew near and we began to wonder where we would be sent to do our missionary work. One day I had an interview with the good bishop and said to him, "I am getting a bit anxious and would like to know what sort of work you are going to give me to do. During the term I have, as you know, visited most of the fairly easily accessible settlements and small towns to take services at the week-ends and I have made up my mind that I want to do some pioneering. I do hope you won't send me to some little town near the city. I want to go up into the north country." The bishop laughed in his quiet, jolly fashion and replied, "Very well: Very well: I will see that you go to some pioneer place if that is what you want."

The following morning the list of men and the missionary areas to which they were to go was posted in the college hall. An excited group of men were gathered round, and when I could get sufficiently near I ran my finger down the list, which was typed in the usual orderly Saskatchewan manner, until I came to my own name near the bottom:
"TAYLOR, R.M. – YANKEE BEND"

I had never heard of 'Yankee Bend'. I sought information from the other men, but none of them seemed to have heard of such a place. I was tempted to go along to see the bishop to find out more about Yankee Bend, but I knew him too well. He is a military type of man, who does not suffer fools gladly. When he told a man to do something it was a sort of 'message-to-Garcia' business, and, if one was wise, one did not ask the bishop foolish questions about a matter so unimportant as the geographical situation of a place. I discovered from the Revd. Henry Wallace, who was then the diocesan secretary-treasurer and another of God's saints if there ever was one) that Yankee Bend was probably north of the town of Lloydminster, across the north

Saskatchewan river and east of the meridian which forms the border-line of the Provinces of Saskatchewan and Alberta.

The name 'Yankee Bend' became quite a huge joke around the College and one evening I returned to find an amazing spectacle in my room. In my absence my colleagues had erected a dummy horse, on it was placed my new English pigskin riding saddle. In the saddle was an effigy of myself, dressed in my own riding kit. [In due course Richard was to be subjected to much ridicule from his future brothers-in-law about this saddle, which they dubbed a 'pancake', because of its size and uselessness for spending many hours on horseback and for working with cattle]. In the room there was also put up a tent made of my blankets, pinned to the top of it was a large card bearing the inscription, 'Yankee Bend Rectory'. I remember how Archdeacon Paul laughed (a rare thing for him to do) when he was brought up to inspect this arrangement. Early the next morning the Bishop addressed us and gave us his advice and his blessing in a voice which trembled with emotion. And so our little company split up, north, south, east and west, out into the bush.

Lloydminster is a town which straddles the border between the provinces of Alberta and Saskatchewan. The Meridian actually runs down the centre of the main street; therefore half of the town lies within the province of Alberta and the other in the province of Saskatchewan. The citizen who liked his glass of beer found this line of demarcation a great convenience when the authorities of Saskatchewan closed the beer parlours and saloons, for he was able, by crossing the main street, to enter Alberta and drink beer to his heart's content. It is a busy little town of two or three thousand inhabitants and serves the needs of a great area of the north country. The settlers bring their grain to the elevators, their cattle to the station and take the opportunity of doing their shopping and trading and of getting a glimpse of the 'white lights'.

The place was named Lloydminster in honour of Bishop George Exton Lloyd who, as a young clergyman and the father of a family, had homesteaded there many years before.

The story of the Barr Colonists is well known. An enterprising (possibly criminal?) clergyman named Isaac Barr persuaded a number of English and Irish people, and their families, to leave the Old Land and settle in the great

Northwest. He gathered around him men, women and children, who left Liverpool and Belfast full of high hopes and dreams of the homes and fortunes they were going to make in the land of plenty, for Barr had painted a glowing picture, with a somewhat liberal hand, of the life that was opening out before them. But alas! We have to record the dismal fact that Barr deserted his company of adventurers. After the ship sailed, Barr was not to be found, and great panic seized the company. Happily for them, the Revd George Exton Lloyd was on board the same ship going out to Canada for the first time to engage in missionary work. In him they found a man with the initiative and courage to help them in their great distress and from that moment he took charge of the expedition

The Revd. Mr. Kuhring, a parson at Halifax, received an urgent message from Mr Lloyd as the ship drew near: - 'Please prepare sixty packets of tea, sugar, condensed milk, flour, biscuits and some bacon and meat, and have them ready for us when we land'. Mr Kuhring, his wife and a company of busy workers, laboured night and day making up these packages to meet the insistent demand of George Lloyd. When the boat arrived in the dock it was he who made all the arrangements for transportation on the railway. The company of settlers-to-be were marshalled on the platform and went to their appointed seats in the colonists' cars on the train. There was no sign of panic or distress as the engine pulled out with the long line of coaches and freight cars out on the first stage of the long journey across the continent to the prairies.

In a little less than a week's time they reached the small settlement, now the thriving city of Saskatoon, and there lived in tents whilst their energetic new leader made further arrangements with the government for the settling of these people, who had left their homes on the other side of the world.

Many of the colonists had money and unscrupulous farm-implement dealers sold them a great deal of expensive and useless machinery, for the watchful eye of Mr. Lloyd could not be everywhere. The men who thus so readily parted with their money little realised that it would be a long time before reaping machinery could be used on the virgin prairie to which they were going. Horses and oxen were at a premium, for there was no railway to take them further. Many a broken-winded old nag changed hands at a price that would have warmed the heart of a vendor of thoroughbred Arabs.

The long trek north-west began. One has heard that much of the newly acquired machinery was gladly discarded after a few days' journey over the tortuous Indian trail. Eventually the company, tired, weary, bedraggled and hungry, reached that piece of almost bald prairie just south of the north Saskatchewan River, which is now the town of Lloydminster and the surrounding district. It was with relief that the tents were erected for the first time. As the men, women and children, gathered around a big camp-fire and ate their evening meal, they must have found it very hard to realise that the very spot on which they were encamped would become their home.

The following morning, after breakfast, Mr. Lloyd gathered his people together and talked to them. He told them that the government surveyor was coming up to mark out the sections of land which were to be allotted to each family, and warned them of the long days of toil which lay ahead. He said there would be toil and tears and sweat in good measure.

In the days and weeks that followed there was much activity. Rude log shacks, with roofs made of poplar saplings, covered with tar-paper, were built and the women soon transformed them into real homes. Mr. Lloyd remained with them and kept alive the spirits of the colonists. Hardships and sickness they had in plenty and many, thoroughly disgusted and disheartened, returned to the British Isles. Those who remained, after years of hard work clearing the land, have done well and are amongst the more prosperous farmers in the Lloydminster district at the present time. They have exchanged their shacks for spacious and well-built houses, with electric light and such up-to-date conveniences as are still the dream of dwellers in rural England.

Mrs Lloyd has spoken to me of some of her experiences in the little shack which was her home in the new settlement; of how the rain came through the roof of turf, soaking everything and everybody underneath it, and of how she found it necessary at times to put her children under the table, which was the only dry space.

The spiritual needs of the colonists were not neglected. It was not long before George Lloyd was making arrangements for services and religious instruction. Soon a little log church made its appearance and regular services were begun in it. He has told me of the joy with which they received the first church organ ever to come into the district – a small American one; of how it came up along the trail all the way from Saskatoon, and how carefully it was unloaded. The following week they had an organ recital in the church. I am sorry to say that the little log church, which has been replaced these many years by a substantial brick one, now stands forlorn at the south end of the main street and is used as a storehouse for sacks of flour and sugar.[4]

At midnight on Maundy Thursday (1929) I arrived at Lloydminster and walked along the deserted streets to the little wooden rectory. Canon Cross, the rector, appeared at the door and bade me enter. I told him that I had been sent by the bishop to open up a mission at Yankee Bend. He replied, "Dear me! I've never heard of the place. It is probably north of the river. However, we needn't worry about that for the moment for you are going to stay where you are until after Easter. Afterward it might be a good idea if you went up to Henry Ellis, the Principal of the Onion Lake Indian School, for he knows that country up north far better than any other man, for I must confess that, although I happen to be the Rural Dean of these parts, I have never heard of the name Yankee Bend until this moment".

At the break of day on Easter Monday morning, Canon Cross took me over to the Royal George Hotel, where it had been arranged that I should meet Percy Taylor, the man responsible for the transportation of His Majesty's mail from Lloydminster to Onion Lake. There I was introduced to mine host and his wife – Mr and Mrs William Smith. I was quick to notice that they both spoke with an accent which immediately betrayed their origin to me, a Derbyshire man myself. I said, "Well, Mr Smith, from what part of Derbyshire do you come, for I am a Derbyshire man myself?" "Well, I'm jiggered", he replied, "Me and my missus come from a little village called Heath, near Chesterfield. I was born and brought up on the farm near the parish church and my wife's home was the Elm Tree Inn". They were surprised to learn that my home was only two miles away from their old village. Thus began a friendship which was one of the bright spots of my sojourn in the north.

---

[4] When I passed through Lloydminster in 1957 I was glad to observe that this building had been rescued and made into a museum commemorating the vicissitudes of those early colonists. W.T.

THE RIVER GOES ON

Promptly at eight o'clock, the tinkle of sleigh bells was to be heard heralding the arrival of the mail man and his sleigh. I climbed aboard and made myself tolerably comfortable among the sacks of mail and away we went at a brisk trot. It was a crisp, bright morning and one felt that it was good to be alive. During the day we made several halts at the farms and ranches to deliver mail. At each halt our horses were fed and we were glad to thaw out around the wood-burning fire and enjoy the good food which the code of hospitality, rigidly observed by the pioneers, ordains shall be set before the wayfarer – without question and without charge.

The corners of the miscellaneous packages in the mail bags, which had been my cushions throughout the day's drive, had found all the tender portions of my anatomy by the time I climbed down, with some relief, from my perch when we reached the south bank of the north Saskatchewan River and found Mr and Mrs Hewitt awaiting the arrival of the mail. The horses were taken into a barn and given a feed for their day's work, because a fresh team would be required to complete the journey. After supper it was soon time to be setting out on the last lap and one felt a little reluctant to depart from the nearness of the glowing stove. "All aboard", shouted Percy, and away we sped down the trail. We crossed the frozen river, which must be at least half a mile wide at this point, climbed the steep banks on the other side and hit the trail for Onion Lake.

This district has a very sandy soil and is therefore only sparsely settled: it is therefore very much as it was when the war-like Indians used the very trail over which we were driving. Some attempts had been made in years past to cultivate the land, but we passed a number of log shacks, pathetic in their roofless condition.

I shall ever remember the drive from the river to Onion Lake. It was very cold – piercingly cold – and the temperature was round about thirty-five degrees below zero. There was a beautiful moon and the northern lights flashing and moving about the sky made a picture of heavenly grandeur which even now makes me catch my breath as memory brings back the glory of it all - the lone spruce trees pointing skyward; the crunch and whistle of the dry snow under the steel runners of the sleigh; the tinkle of the bells on the horses; the mournful baying of the coyotes in the distance; and, over all, I was filled with an exhilarating sense of adventure as I anticipated the future new life, which was already unfolding before me. As we slid along at a good pace behind our fresh horses, I lay on my back amongst the mail-bags and meditated upon the changes the past few months had brought into my life.

We reached St. Barnabas Anglican Indian Residential School at ten o'clock that night and what a surprise I had! There in the midst of that wilderness I found the most modern and up-to-date Church of England school – beautiful buildings and the most comfortable principal's house, standing in a cultivated plateau above the lake. For over seventy years the Church has cared for the Indian folk up here. The first school was a simple log building built by Mr Matheson, a pioneer missionary, who was priest, teacher, doctor, guide, counsellor and friend to the original warlike Cree Indians. At the new school some hundred Indian boys and girls live for the greater part of each year. They receive a first-class and practical education. Apart from the usual school subjects, the boys are taught to farm and have the advantage of learning on a model farm with good stock and all sorts of up-to-date farming equipment and electricity. The girls are also taught to keep house, to sew, to cook and prepare themselves to be good mothers.

I was greeted at the school by the Principal, the Revd. Henry Ellis, who for many years has done wonderful work in this remote part of the North West. There I met Mrs Ellis, that wonderful woman, who is his wife and partner – the mother of a large family, with a heart of gold, and with enough love to spare for the stranger, the wanderer and the sad at heart. I am glad, out of gratitude, to pay tribute to them. Certainly I shall never be able to repay them for all they did for me in those early years in the West, for their home was my home, their table was my table, and they gave me encouragement, sympathy and advice.

5 Historical Background

The territory into which Richard travelled in the early part of 1929 was once named Rupert's Land. It formed a small part of an enormous area stretching from Hudson Bay, over the Rocky Mountains into what later became British Columbia which was granted in 1670 to Prince Rupert, a cousin of Charles ll.

> 'Rupert and 17 associates obtained from the King their incorporation as **The Governor and Company of Adventurers of England trading into Hudson's Bay** . . It is by far the most far-reaching commercial document in British history (and) in sheer spaciousness the grant has never been equalled, except by such fairyland dreams as the grant of Pope Alexander VI dividing the New World half in half between Spain and Portugal . . . But the charter went even beyond Rupert's Land. Where their own government ended the Company were to have the right of trade in all "the havens, bays, creeks, rivers, lakes and seas" into which they could find passage from their own area'.[5]

The sheer effrontery of this audacious document leaves us gasping: no mention whatsoever is made of the rights of those indigenous inhabitants, whom we shall call 'Indians' for want of a better word, who had already occupied the land for centuries[6]. The arrival of the Adventurers and their descendants was to have tragic consequences for them. Nonetheless, one can only admire the courage and resourcefulness of those early travellers and explorers, in whose path Richard felt that he was following.

The province of Saskatchewan had been carved out of Rupert's Land territory in 1905, only 24 years before Richard arrived on the scene. Stretching from the 49th parallel in the south, along the border with the United States, it was traversed by the two branches of the Saskatchewan River, North and South, which flowed east into the network of lakes and rivers to the north of Fort Garry, or Winnipeg, as it was later called. Thus the river formed the natural means of communication into the North West territories for the early voyageurs and fur-traders. Indeed, it was the principal river

---

[5] *Canada. The foundations of its future.* Stephen Leacock. pp. 76,77.
[6] *Native Peoples and Cultures of Canada.* Alan D. McMillan. p.1. (NPCC)

of the fur-trade in Western Canada. Initially it had many other names – 'La Riviere Blanche', because of the white water rapids at the Grand Rapids: or 'Red Deer River' – but Saskatchewan is a Cree word meaning 'swift flowing'. Initially the prairies were the background to much bitter rivalry between the Hudson's Bay Company and the Montreal-based North West Company. The land was dotted with forts, which sprang up as each fur company pushed westward. But in 1821 the two companies finally agreed to merge. Fort Pitt was built in 1829, shortly after the merger, on the north shore of the Saskatchewan. It was named after Thomas Pitt, a member of the London Committee from 1810 to 1832. Situated on the river bench, which was a favourite spot for travellers on the Saskatchewan, its position was not ideal, as the tragic events of the 1885 rebellion were to prove so vividly. The bank of the river is usually about 20 feet above low water level. From this bank there is a flat extending back for some 100 yards and then there is a rise of another 20 or 30 feet to the bench. On this bench the traders built their fort, but beyond it by as much as half a mile was the valley wall. There was therefore no well for water; the Fort's inhabitants had to depend on river water, and they were vulnerable to attack from the hill to the north behind them.

During the winter of 1912 –13 a crew built a ferry on the bank of the north Saskatchewan River (about 4 to 5 miles downstream).

> *It was known as Yankee Bend ferry until the railway came in 1928, when the Canadian National Railway named the hamlet Frenchman Butte, after a geographical feature that rises about four hundred feet above the average terrain and is the second highest point of land in Saskatchewan. The name Frenchman was tacked on as a Frenchman had been trading there prior to the Hudson's Bay or Northwest fur traders.[7]*

But the river was not the only means of travel into the remoter regions of north Saskatchewan. Before the arrival of the river steamers, the early settlers had made their way laboriously into the so-called 'Fertile Belt' that lay across the two tributaries of the Saskatchewan in what were called 'Red River carts'.

---

[7] *Fort Pitt History Unfolding.* p. 205.

To cross the North West, in the early days before the railway, was a considerable feat attempted by only a hardy few. The chief form of transportation was by Red River cart, "scrub oak shaganappi and squeals," as John McDougall, the pioneer Fort Edmonton trader called them. The carts, pulled by oxen, were adapted from Scottish vehicles – light boxes, each perched on a single axle with wheels six feet high. There was one difference: they contained not a single nail, nor, indeed a scrap of iron. Instead, tough strands of buffalo hide – the all-purpose "shaganappi" – were used. The axles could not be greased because the thick prairie dust would quickly immobilise the carts; as a result the wheels emitted an infernal screeching, "the North West fiddle," as some pioneers dubbed it.

The carts left deep ruts in the soft prairie turf, so deep that the wagons tended to spread out, the right wheel of one cart travelling in the wake of the left wheel of the cart ahead; thus the prairie trails could be as much as twenty carts wide, a phenomenon that helps explain the broad streets of some of the pioneer towns.

These trails furrowed the plains like the creases on a human palm. . . The most famous trail of all was the Carlton Trail, the aorta of the plains, winding for 1,160 miles from Fort Garry (Winnipeg) to the Yellow Head Pass in the Rockies by way of Fort Carlton and Fort Edmonton. It was slow going to travel that famous thoroughfare. It took a good forty days for an ox cart to negotiate the initial 479 miles to Fort Carlton. For half a century this was the broad highway used by every explorer, settler, trader or adventurer who set his sights for the West.[8]

The Carlton trail was to play a significant part in the history of the Pepper family. A section of it, between Battleford and Fort Pitt before heading west to Edmonton, was known as the 'Fort Pitt' or 'Battleford Trail'. Along it, from Edam to Fort Pitt, came Fred Pepper with his wife, Daisy, and their children, Grace, Rose, Nat, the triplets – Charlie, Harvey and John – Lloyd, Peggy (Margaret), Mildred, James, Kathleen and Bill in 1924, after all attempts to farm

---

[8] *The National Dream.* Pierre Berton. pp. 44,45.

the sandy soil around Edam had ended in failure. In any case, Fred was anxious to revert to his true forte i.e. horses. By moving on to Fort Pitt they were therefore following in the tracks of those early 'homesteaders' whose dream it was to open up the west.

The story of Fort Pitt itself is inevitably linked with that of the Saskatchewan Rebellion on 1885, when the Indians and the Métis[9] made common cause against the perceived oppression of the government. Fort Pitt was in "No Man's Land" in those days, an important port of call on the river, a trading post where pemmican[10] from the adjacent prairies and a few beaver brought in by the Wood Crees were exchanged for other goods. It also stood as a frontier post between those deadly and hereditary enemies – the Crees and the Blackfoot Indians.

With the transfer of the title to the Northwest from the Hudson's Bay Company to Canada, treaties were concluded with both tribes and soon nearly all of them were located on their allocated reserves. With the prairies cleared of the roaming marauders an influx of settlers took place. The new railway spanning the plains cut through the heart of the Blackfoot country and, at the same time, the buffalo disappeared forever. The Indians who had signed the treaty, but had not yet accepted the restrictions imposed by confinement on reserves, experienced actual distress; those who still held out against treaty were destitute.

In this confused situation the Métis turned to the leader of their previous abortive revolution in 1870, Louis Riel, now living in exile in the United States. As before, a provisional government was proclaimed, at Batoche near Prince Albert, but this time, despite gaps in the rail link with the east, troops could be quickly moved to the scene of the uprising.

The first skirmish took place near Duck Lake (between Batoche and Fort Carlton), where the North West Mounted Police arrived to assert

---

[9] The Métis (from a French word meaning 'mixed') emerged as products of the fur trade, the offspring of European men and native women. Although the term can be applied to anyone of mixed racial heritage, it came primarily to refer to those who forged a common identity on the plains of Western Canada in the 19th Century. NPCC page 273.

[10] An important source of food made out of dried buffalo meat, pounded into powder and mixed with berries and any available fat.

the authority of the Dominion of Canada. The Métis, with a few Indians from nearby reserves, controlled the surrounding woods. Ten police soon lay dead upon the ground and the rest were forced to flee. The Métis would have pursued them and inflicted greater casualties, but were forbidden by Riel. This defeat caused the police to abandon Fort Carlton and move to the larger settlement of Prince Albert.

News of the Métis victory at Duck Lake spread quickly among the Indian camps. Messengers from Riel urged them to join in common cause with their Métis kin. Disillusioned with the treaties, chafing under the restraints of life on their reserves and starving due to misguided government restraint policy, many Indians were eager to join the rebellion. Several hundred Cree besieged the fort at Battleford, looting and burning surrounding homes and stores. There they were joined by Assiniboines, who had left their reserve after killing their farm instructor and a settler. Further to the northwest, the Cree warriors of Big Bear's band killed the Indian agent, two priests and six others at Frog Lake and forced the abandonment of Fort Pitt, which they pillaged and burned.

It was the shock of the deaths at Frog Lake that forced the government to act decisively. While the Métis had not caused a great deal of government concern, the spectre of a general Indian uprising across the west certainly did. Troops were hastily dispatched, dividing into a three-pronged assault on the insurgents. One column headed after Big Bear's Cree, while another proceeded to relieve Battleford, and the main force moved against the Métis capital of Batoche.

The final outcome of the Battle of Batoche could never have been in doubt. A few hundred Métis with smooth-bore muzzle-loaders were no match for nearly a thousand soldiers with rifles, cannons and the rapid-fire Gatling gun. Métis supplies of ammunition were low, and by the end of the conflict many were reduced to firing nails and pebbles. Nevertheless, deeply dug into rifle pits and trenches, the Métis held off the military onslaught for four days. Finally, the rifle pits were overrun, and the Métis defenders fled to the woods.

Riel agreed to surrender . . to continue to plead the cause of the Métis to the government of Canada. The trials which followed sent a number of Métis and Indians to prison. . Eight Cree and Assiniboine were hanged at Battleford for the murders in 1885.[11]

At the time of its abandonment to the combined forces of the Métis and the Indians, the garrison at Fort Pitt was commanded by no less a person than Inspector Francis Dickens, one of the sons of the famous author, Charles Dickens. After a varied career, that had included a spell with the Bengal Police, he found himself in northern Saskatchewan. In many ways he was a sad, somewhat inadequate person, always conscious of failing to live up to his father's expectations: partially deaf, he was afflicted with a strong stammer. His part in the struggle which took place at Fort Pitt is well described by that radical exponent of Scottish history, John Prebble, whose own childhood was spent in Saskatchewan at about the same time as Fred and Daisy were raising their large family at Edam and Fort Pitt. In his autobiography he writes:

> *The Canadian West was still a young country when I was a boy, and its mind did not dwell long on the immediate past. Yet the spring campaign against Poundmaker and Big Bear of the Crees, against Louis Riel and Gabriel Dumont, the political and military leaders of the Métis, had passed over the ground where our little settlement [of Sutherland] would be built within twenty years.*

> *I am aware that a boy's imagination might not have made improving use of the knowledge, but I wish I had known then that the old prairie-trail which became Main Street, Sutherland, had been ridden by Inspector Francis Dickens and his detachment of mounted constables during the Riel Rebellion. Red-haired and red-bearded, partly deaf and a stammerer, he was forty-one and in the last year of his life. He had been unadmired and perhaps unloved by his father. Charles Dickens had no faith in him, no confidence that he would achieve, and like other men who have themselves achieved he perhaps saw his children's failure as his own. In his youth, Francis asked his father for £15, a horse and a gun, that he might go abroad and farm. Refusing the request, Dickens argued that his son would be robbed of the money,*

---

[11] NPCC pages 282 – 285.

thrown from the horse, and blow out his brains with the gun. Escaping from the journalist's stool upon which his father placed him, Francis Dickens finally went abroad, first to the Bengal Police, and then halfway about the globe to the North West Mounted.

Before the outbreak of the Riel Rebellion he was sent northward to the Cree country with twenty constables. He crossed the south fork of the Saskatchewan at Saskatoon, then little more than a scattering of sod and timber shacks, and rode to the north fork and the garrison of Fort Pitt beyond the Eagle Hills. This was both a police station and a trading-post, with its own Highland piper and a stout pier for the voyagers' canoes and the big flat-bottomed boats of the Hudson's Bay Company. It was soon a refuge for alarmed settlers, driven in by the news that the Crees under Big Bear had pillaged a settlement at Frog Lake and killed eight white men, including a priest at the altar. The Indians soon arrived about Fort Pitt with a band of armed Métis, cutting all escape or access except by the eastward stream of the river. With little food or ammunition, a defence of the fort was impossible, and Dickens drove his constables and the fugitives into the building of a large scow by which they might go downriver. Ice was still moving when the leaky vessel was finished, lurching floes grinding against each other or rising like up-thrust spears from a swirl of black water and earth-brown foam. Travelling for a week, crouching beneath occasional rifle-fire from the banks and expecting the scow to founder at every cruel twist of the river, the party of sixty men and women finally reached the tall trees and raw timber walls of the fort at Battleford. It was truly an achievement for Inspector Dickens, and might have seemed so to his father, if belatedly, and had the novelist been alive.[12]

[The site of the old Fort Pitt has been restored in recent years, being marked on the maps as 'The Fort Pitt Provincial Historic Park', which was opened in 1973 and the land nearby is occupied by a Hutterian Brethren Colony].

A significant factor in the rapid collapse of the rebellion was that the Canadian Pacific Railway across the continent was

---

[12] *Landscapes and Memories.* John Prebble. pp. 183,184.

nearing completion. There were gaps in the route, especially north of Lake Superior, which were traversed with considerable difficulty; troops, supplies and reinforcements, with volunteers eager to join in the fight – among them Exton Lloyd, later Bishop of Saskatchewan – soon arrived.

In 'The Book of the West' H.A. Kennedy describes in vivid detail the Frog Lake massacre, when 'Nine men in all were shot, including two priests . . only the Hudson's Bay clerk was spared'. This book is now in my possession, but Richard had it with him at Fort Pitt in 1931 and he comments in the margin (page 101), "This was W. Bleasdale Cameron, who has stayed with me several times at Fort Pitt Mission House".

One of the long-term results of the debacle at Fort Pitt was its rapid decline as a trading-post. Two years later, in June 1887, the man in charge, Angus McKay, wrote to his chief factor at Prince Albert,

> The location of Fort Pitt as a centre of trade for this district has become unsuitable, and that of Onion Lake more desirable, owing to changes brought about by the rebellion. The Frog Lake and Long Lake Indian reserves have been abandoned by the Government and the Onion Lake reserve supported only. The result is that comparatively few families from the abandoned places are now at large hunting to support themselves – of the rest, some have gone out of Treaty as Halfbreeds and the others have moved on to the Onion Lake reserve. Thus while thinning the population of Indian hunters from the outlying district – that of Onion Lake is increasing. And here too the Indian Agency, Mounted Police and Trading Firm are located. By establishing at Onion Lake, the traders are twelve miles nearer than we are to the Indian hunters of the surrounding country and are also in a position to deprive us of the custom to be derived from the Indian Department employees, Police and Reserve Indians. I would therefore strongly advise that we also establish ourselves permanently at Onion Lake.[13]

---

[13] FPH page 104.

At Onion Lake there were two Christian missions, Roman Catholic and Anglican, between whom there was fierce rivalry for the 'souls' of the Indians. Naturally Richard was glad to arrive at the latter at Eastertide 1929, relieved to find a friendly welcome from its principal, the Revd. Henry Ellis. With the gift of hindsight, it is easy to marvel at his naivety at accepting the wonders of the institution. But before we move on to the story of his subsequent pioneering work among the white settlers in the Fort Pitt area, how he met and married Peggy (Margaret) Pepper, and built several churches, all in the short spell of three years, we need to remember what life was like for those Indian children, taken away from their families, to be "civilized" in residential schools such as that at Onion Lake, especially in the light of recent reports of abuse and harsh treatment. Ivan MacDonald (a Cree Indian) who enrolled at Onion Lake School in 1928, at the age of four, writes of his experiences,

> 'these residential schools' main function was "the eradication of the Indian child's cultural heritage". The parents were forced to sign an agreement making the school's principal the legal guardian of the children . . . I did not go home for the summer holidays until I was eight years old and so I did not understand very much Cree. At least seven per cent of former pupils of these residential schools were sick or in poor health . . . I had two older brothers who contracted TB . . they both died within ten years of leaving. . . Our life at the school was governed by the bell and endless line ups . . I don't know how I forgot to tell about the number we received when we first got to school. . . this stayed with us until we left. I was number 31 for 14 years. Allen Sapp, the famous painter, was number 33.[14]

---

[14] FPH page 158.

6 Peggy and the Peppers

Peggy was Fred's first daughter by Daisy. Her birth certificate is a remarkable document. It was not issued until December 1947 when Peggy, or Margaret as she was always known after her marriage, was preparing to make her one, solitary, return trip to Canada before Richard died. In it the place of her birth has no name, just a grid reference on the map: 33 – 48 – 20 – W 3rd. SASK. This defined an isolated settlement, called Edam, situated on the line of the Battleford Trail as it follows the Turtlelake River NW of Battleford. As its name suggests, most of the other settlers were Dutch emigrants.

Fred, while living at Swan Lake in Manitoba, had been granted the land at Edam by the Saskatchewan provincial government to celebrate the birth in 1908 of the triplets, Charles, Harvey and John, together with the arrival, one year later, in June 1909, of another son, Lloyd. Shortly beforehand, in 1905, the province of Saskatchewan had been defined as part of the Dominion of Canada and the need for settlers and homesteaders to open up and develop the territory was paramount. Fred was given one square mile, a section (640 acres) with a quarter for himself and each of the triplets, but the fact that the soil at Edam was of poor quality, consisting largely of sand, was something he was to discover later through bitter experience.

Peggy was born on 15th October 1911, the eighth child in a family that was eventually to grow to twelve. With the three children, Grace (1901 – 36), Nat (1903 – 1987), and Rose (1904 -), that he had adopted from Daisy's first marriage, and the arrival, after the birth of Peggy, of Mildred (1915 -), James (1917 – 1940), Kathleen (1918 – 2001) and Bill (1921 -), Fred found himself with the daunting task of raising a large family on a farm, or homestead, based on poor soil. Not surprisingly in 1924 he decided to try his luck further northwest in the province. There, at Fort Pitt, he bought some land, together with a lease on further sections at Bronson Lake to the north, which had first been developed by that extraordinary pioneer and missionary, John Matheson. He had died in 1916, so it was with his widow, Elizabeth Matheson, herself an indomitable frontier doctor and medicine woman, [15] that Fred negotiated the lease on this new land. Many years later my sister, Gillian, recounted, with some glee, the story of Fred's early adventures at Fort Pitt, details of which Peggy, in her 90th year was reluctant to corroborate. It is believed that, in 1924, Fred went on ahead of the family with his brother, to establish a home at Fort Pitt and, in particular, to build some sort of home or ranch. Instead he found himself inveigled into a highly illegal whisky producing operation, supplying the hard-working and hard-living men who were driving roads and railways into the new territory. In due course the attentions of the Mounties discouraged his efforts.

To describe Peggy's father, Fred Pepper, as a resourceful and lively character, is to do him scant justice. He was already 37 when, in 1907, he met and married Daisy Hunt. She was a young widow of 29 who had come out from England the year before, leaving behind in Nottinghamshire her three young children by her first husband, Sam Hunt. What exactly Fred got up to in those thirty-seven years is not easy to discover at this distance in time. A love of horses, an Irish temperament and much travel during those exciting years, when the Canadian west was being opened up for settlement by the construction of railroads, has been a fruitful source of many family legends. In one of them I was told how Fred ran away from home at the age of 15 to fight the Indians at the time of the Riel rebellion in the mid 1880s. Certainly he was a cowboy in the age of cowboys. At the age of 12, in 1882, he had gone west when his father and family moved from Lanark County, Ontario, and settled at Wolseley in Saskatchewan. This was, in the phrase used at the time, 'at the end of the steel': in other words, it was as far as the transcontinental railroad had reached. It was a point some 70 miles east of Regina, which later became the provincial capital of Saskatchewan. In his teens, as his son, Bill, recalled later, "Dad moved around quite a bit". It was a time of turmoil in the Northwest Territories, as they were then described. Quite suddenly and dramatically the herds of buffaloes disappeared from the prairies, massacred in thousands by the settlers and the hungry Indians, for whom for centuries they had been a primary source of

---

[15] Ruth Matheson Buck, *The Doctor rode side-saddle.*

food. [Alan McMillan in his 'Native Peoples and Cultures of Canada' gives us a good description of the connection between the disappearance of the buffalo, the disaffection of the Indians and the Métis, and the links between all three, which culminated in the Riel Rebellion]. The remorseless tentacles of the 'steel' were spreading into the territory, bringing in their wake settlers from eastern Canada, or emigrants from Europe, hungry for land.

For a while Fred, with his brother Ernest, moved south of the border into the United States to farm near Minot in North Dakota. But this was not for long. Soon he moved back into Canada, following the railroad as it moved north-west to Saskatoon. Each spring he started out with a herd of cattle, which he grazed along the line of the railroad to keep the construction crews supplied with fresh meat. Later he moved to Stoney Mountain in Manitoba, where he and his brother, maintained a herd of buffalo that they were trying to save. After some 25 years riding with cattle and buffalo over the vast prairie expanses of Dakota and Saskatchewan, Fred returned to Swan Lake in Manitoba where, in a hotel run by his brother, he met Daisy Hunt and soon afterwards married her.

It was a fruitful union, in every sense of the word. Fred and Daisy were well met and very fond of each other. "Daisy was a marvellous manager", said Peggy years later. Her first husband, Sam Hunt, had been a butcher and she came from a family of market gardeners at Gedling in Nottinghamshire. So she was ideally qualified to raise a large family of twelve children on an isolated ranch in northern Saskatchewan. But before we turn to discover what life was like on that isolated ranch as Peggy grew up we need to retrace the trail of Fred and Daisy's family history insofar as it can be done.

Daisy Pepper was born in 1878 at Gedling in Nottinghamshire, England (i.e. not too far from the birthplace in Derbyshire of Peggy's husband Richard Taylor). She had married Sam Hunt, a butcher, in 1900. He died in 1905, leaving her with three young children: Grace, Rose and Nat. We can only imagine the circumstances that forced her to leave the three children with her mother in England, when she sailed from Liverpool on Thursday June 7th, 1906, in the Allan Line 'Turbine Triple-Screw

Steamer' *Victorian*, bound for Quebec and Montreal. A copy of the ship's manifest bears her name mistakenly as 'Miss D. Hunt', together with that of her sister, 'Miss E. Buxton'. Daisy initially worked in Winnipeg as a doctor's housekeeper, but, when that job folded, she went to be cook in a hotel at Swan Lake where she met Fred. Soon after she married Fred, her three children were able to travel to Canada to join her. We do not know if their arrival coincided with the birth of the triplets, Charles, Harvey and John, on May 18th 1908, or with the birth of Lloyd thirteen months later on June 29th 1909. What we do know is that, 30 months after his marriage as a bachelor at the age of 37, Fred found himself with a family of seven children to care for, to be joined by an eighth child, Peggy, in 1911.

Fred was born, George Frederick, on April 26th 1870 at Palmerston in Lanark County, Ontario, not far from Ottawa. His parents, George (born 17th November 1842) and Catherine (née Walker, born 24th August 1845), both came from Palmerston, Ontario. Catherine died in 1875, when Fred was only five years old, and five years later George married Margaret McQuat, by whom he had five children. So it was that Fred's first daughter, Peggy, bore the names of both his mother and his stepmother – Catherine and Margaret.

George Pepper's parents came from Enniscorthy, County Wexford, in Ireland. His father, William (1800 – 1888) was born at Enniscorthy, but emigrated as a child with his parents, Robert and Jane (née Smith) sometime during the early 1800s. Hence they did not cross the Atlantic as part of the wave of emigrants driven from their home in Ireland by the horrors of the potato famine of the mid 19th Century. They came over earlier in the century, soon after the end of the Napoleonic wars, at much the same time as Eliza Anne Taylor (1810 – 1896; born in Dublin), also emigrated with her parents. The two families settled in Ontario. Eliza later became William's wife. William, having moved to Elizabethtown, established his first home there with Eliza whose parents had first settled in Brockville. Subsequently William and Eliza moved to Oakville and Belleville, also in Ontario, until finally settling in the 2nd County of Lanark, where they are both buried in the Anglican cemetery. In summary, both of Fred's paternal grandparents William and Eliza emigrated from Ireland as children: we do not know when they married or why their parents emigrated from Ireland in the first place.

The earliest photographs we have of Peggy show her, first of all, some few months old, held in her mother's arms, as part of a family group seated proudly in front of the simple frame building that was their home at Edam. It is 1912. The triplets are there, Harvey, Charlie and John, all dressed alike in short trousers, knee-length stockings and heavy boots. At the back are the Hunt children – Grace, Rose and Nat – and Lloyd is there, in front of Fred, who shelters beneath a broad-brimmed hat. He looks unusually solemn for the camera – no doubt aware of and somewhat awed by his numerous responsibilities. A later photograph shows Peggy, at two or three years old, wearing a pinafore over her frock, with Dinah the dog. But these are the only photographs we have of life at Edam. For the rest we must rely on the spoken reminiscences of Peggy shared many years later with myself.

When the Canadian government began to develop the new territories in the west one of its first concerns was to establish a school in each new settlement. These were called 'Cole schools', after the politician who advocated their establishment. They were distinct from the schools provided by the churches and missionaries on the Indian reserves, which, in so many cases, were to have a tragic reputation. Naturally, as Peggy remembered later, the school at Edam was full of Dutch children. Such a place was the centre of community life and to it the children travelled, sometimes many miles, on foot or on horseback. The stable was an integral part of every school and here in winter the sleighs or 'cutters' were kept. Frequently there was just one teacher for the whole school. Here then Peggy received her education until the age of 13, when the family moved to Fort Pitt. By then it was complete: Fred and Daisy, with their twelve children, three Hunts and nine Peppers, the last of whom was Bill, only three years old in 1924.

I have mentioned already how Fred's preparations at Fort Pitt for the family may have been somewhat inadequate. To compound the problem, the journey was fraught with difficulty. The train broke down, thus forcing Fred and the family to complete the journey by horse and wagon along the Battleford Trail. They followed the route carved out of the wilderness by countless settlers before them, which linked the little town of St. Walburg with the mission station and settlement on the Indian reserve at Onion Lake. It was on the reserve that an earlier settler, Jim Morton, had leased land on which he could run cattle. It was this lease, together with the Matheson ranch at Fort Pitt itself, which Fred Pepper took over. "When we arrived at Fort Pitt from Edam on March 24th 1924", said Peggy's sister, Mildred, later, "I was sure, as my brother had told me, that we were near the North Pole". Maybe Mildred was not mistaken in her first impressions.

To travel north from Fort Pitt, as I was to discover for myself in 1957, after 50 miles or so one soon comes to the Beaver River. This drains east, through the countless lakes of the glacial shield country, into Hudson Bay, and thus into the Arctic Ocean.

The Pepper ranch itself was built on the side of a gentle hill facing west and overlooking Pepper Lake and Old Man Creek. The land running south to Yankee Bend and the broad sweep of the north Saskatchewan River had already been broken up for arable farming. Scattered farms or ranches dotted the landscape with, here and there, some still inhabited earth-roofed, timbered shacks, reminders of the more primitive dwellings erected by the first homesteaders. Life was to change with the arrival of the railway in 1928, but in 1924 the situation was much as Inspector Dickens described it when he arrived to take command of the Hudson's Bay Company post, with the barracks of the North West Mounted police, forty years earlier.

'Fort Pitt was important as a port of call (on the north Saskatchewan River), a stopping place in winter and summer. Even in summer, when the mighty brigades of the traders gave colour to the great river, visitors from the east eagerly looked forward to their first glimpse of Fort Pitt as the dividing line between prairie and northern forest. They were amply repaid in their expectations. Sweeping around a curve in the river one met a scene of beauty: the broad waters lapping the flat on the north bank carried the eye beyond the gradually rising land clothed with thick aspen and poplar brush, intermingled with the rich green of the spruce that signalled the end of monotonous prairie;

the south shore, with its regular rising terraces, was almost park-like at first glance – a scene of peaceful charm'[16]

Life on the Pepper ranch reflected this dividing line between prairie and northern forest, with arable crops grown on what was left of the prairie and cattle grazing in clearings hacked out of the forest. But to call the Pepper home a 'ranch' is perhaps to give a false impression. Initially it was a simple, basic, square, timber house with four rooms and a long verandah running down one side. Underneath was a large cellar in which food and fuel was stored. Subsequently two further rooms were added. Inside were two large bedrooms and two living rooms, one of which was the kitchen. Lighting came from oil lamps – there was no electricity or running water, no bathroom and only an outside toilet, a visit to which was a cold and hasty process in winter. "We were like a herd of mice bundled in together", Peggy recalled later, "with three in a bed the first winter". Two stoves provided warmth – a large cooker in the kitchen, with the other in the corner of the living room. It was a continuing job to keep the fire stoked. In the morning it was Fred's task to get up first, stoke up the stove and make a pot of tea. Then a cup was taken through to Daisy, who didn't get up early, but usually waited to have her breakfast while the others washed up.

During the long, intensely cold Saskatchewan winter, life revolved around those stoves. It was a "terror to get out of bed" into a room where the inside of the windows were covered with ice formed by frozen breath. For entertainment and occupation the women would knit, sew, or crochet: the boys, with Fred, would play card games. There were some books and the weekly edition of the Winnipeg Free Press, delivered on Fridays, provided news of the outside world. Mail arrived in the settlement twice a week, on Wednesdays and Saturdays. Of course there was no TV and not even a radio, except a primitive crystal set, with which Charlie constantly tinkered, producing "raucous sounds but no news or entertainment".

But it would be a mistake to imagine that life was grim. Certainly it was hard, but shining through Peggy's subsequent

---

[16] FPH page 75.

recollections is a strong sense of family unity, based on Fred and Daisy's love for each other and the deep affection between all the siblings, mingled with natural rivalry and an Irish sense of fun and mischief.

Fred with the boys ran the farm and horses, while Daisy managed the home, where her training as the daughter of a market-gardener and her knowledge of how to handle meat, acquired from her first husband, stood the family in good stead. It was against this background that Peggy grew up from the girl of 13, who arrived at Fort Pitt in 1924, to the young woman of 17, who greeted Richard Taylor when he first visited the ranch in 1929.

As one can imagine, such a life was dominated by the rhythm of the seasons. During winter, survival depended upon staying warm and keeping the cattle fed, while food for the family was produced by provisions carefully grown, harvested and preserved during the summer and autumn. Wagg's store provided everything else except clothes which, if not sewn or knitted at home, came by mail order from Timothy Eaton or Robert Simpson, the big department stores in Toronto and Montreal.

Two abiding memories of Peggy are connected with the laborious task of washing clothes for such a large family and the preparation of meat. Peggy herself was largely responsible for the washing because her two elder half-sisters, Grace and Rose, soon left the home to seek employment elsewhere. So she, as the eldest daughter, had to cope with the enormous weekly laundry, using a home-made soap made of lard and lye.[17] "By the time I had finished the weekly washing each week the skin had peeled from my hands". And when the need for meat arose Fred would say to the boys, "Let's go get us a steer", or the local beef-ring or co-operative would slaughter a beast, sharing out the meat between the various members of the group. Then Daisy, with Peggy, would find themselves faced with the task of dealing with a large portion of dead beef, laid upon the kitchen table. "Mother was so good at using all the innards, the bits and bobs, even the sweetbreads, whatever they are. She made wonderful sausages and brawn. Her bread was lovely".

---

[17] Lye – alkalized water made by the lixiviation of vegetable ashes – any strong alkaline solution, especially one used for washing. (OED).

There were other sources of food. Fred loved his pigs and even in winter fish could be caught through a hole cut in the ice, with bait suspended from a "jigger" that wiggled its way under the frozen surface of the water. They mostly caught whitefish, which were either eaten fresh or, when cooked in salt and vinegar, could be preserved in jars and later eaten whole like sardines.

By early April spring began to arrive. No longer would it be possible to cross over the frozen north Saskatchewan River to pick up the trail to Lloydminster and, until the river was clear of ice, the ferry was also out of action. Then the warm "chinook" wind brought with it the long-awaited thaw and suddenly there was a frantic rush to get the crops and vegetables into the ground. With a single plough Fred broke up the garden soil before Daisy, with all the family help she could muster, got cracking with her beloved garden. Potatoes, carrots, turnips, cabbages, rhubarb, beans and peas – anything that could flourish in the short Canadian growing season. Then came the task of preserving as many of these vegetables as possible, until the cellar beneath the house was filled with produce: the shelves full of sealed jars, cabbages and onions hanging from the floor above, and potatoes carefully stored to preserve them from light and frost. Fish, beef and chickens were cut, cooked and packed in salt in sealed jars, the jars standing eight at a time in the washing boiler. With such a large family to feed nothing could be wasted.

Nor were members of the family the only people to cater for. As the youngsters grew up there would be guests and friends to feed or put up overnight on the sofa in the living-room. Folk would come to 'visit' in the Canadian fashion and thus might stay for hours or days – the arrival of a visitor in the midst of the lonely life of the prairie was a welcome event. When there was a dance at the local hall Peggy would sometimes have to wash and iron as many as seven white shirts for her seven brothers. The famous Frenchman Butte stampede, which first took place in the summer of 1932, just after Peggy and Richard had left the community, reflects the vigour, vitality and sheer fun of prairie life, even at the height of the depression. When she described the event later, Edna Lifesco wrote: 'On this occasion Fred volunteered the use of his cattle for competitive cow-walking, calf-roping and steer-riding'. 'Characters such as Slim Hendershied came in from the bush looking for a horse to ride'. 'Lloyd', who shared his father's deep love of horses, 'soon bounced off one in a graceful arc, to land on his seat in the mud', while 'with rain running down every fold of his yellow slicker, Fred Pepper had the time of his life'. 'In the evening Harvey carried his phonograph over to a nearby barn, and the crowd danced the night away in the big empty loft'.[18]

Such was the background of Peggy's life as she left school at the age of 15 in 1926. For two years she continued to escort her younger brothers and sisters to school, managing the horses, or driving the sleigh. She loved reading novels and poetry and from time to time she assisted the teacher with supervision and the easier lessons. But soon domestic chores at home and life on the ranch became her chief occupation with an important role at the heart of the family as Fred and Daisy's eldest daughter.

Photographs of her, taken at this time, portray a slim, lovely and maybe rather shy young woman, with the kind smile that was so to captivate Richard's heart when he arrived on the scene in 1929. Their own four daughters, in later years, would replicate that image. But to say this is to anticipate events. Having discovered how Richard made his own journey to Saskatchewan, and learnt something of what life for Peggy was like at that time, we must now learn how the two of them met and fell in love.

---

[18] FPH pages 224,225.

7 Fort Pitt 1929 - 32.

In December 1928, as Richard was about to begin his journey to Canada, members of the Anglican National Commission made a visit to the district around Fort Pitt and Frenchman Butte, where the settlers had asked to have a missionary and the ministrations of the Church. As a result of these developments Richard received his call to go to 'Yankee Bend' and later to return to Bishop's College, Prince Albert, for further study and training during the winters of 1929/30 and 30/31. This was to be his only formal preparation for the ministry. But in those early years what he lacked in formal qualifications was more than compensated for by a powerful sense of 'calling' and a dogged determination, coupled with sheer courage, that enabled him to surmount the formidable obstacles that lay ahead of him.

Having stayed with the Ellis family at the Onion Lake School, Richard reached Fort Pitt soon after Easter 1929; there he preached to a congregation of twelve, who had assembled in an old log building for divine service. We cannot know for certain if any representatives of the Pepper family were in the congregation: Margaret recalls later that most of the children were suffering from measles at the time and Daisy, her mother, had just returned from a visit to England, where her father, Nathaniel Buxton, had just died. But it seems probable that Richard's basic medical skills, which were part of his training at Bishop's College, and the chance of a friendly reception from a fellow exile from the English Midlands, made an early call on the Pepper ranch more than likely.

When Richard arrived in 1929 he was appalled to discover that there was no consecrated ground where the settlers could bury their dead, the nearest cemetery being at Onion Lake, nearly 20 miles away. Soon Mr William Taylor, a churchwarden, donated for this purpose, two acres of land, situated not far from the Pepper ranch. [Confusingly the name William Taylor will continually appear throughout this narrative, being held by Richard's father, both churchwardens at Fort Pitt and Mindemoya and myself]. At two meetings, held in the store, a simple log building which also did duty as post office and general meeting-place, the settlers decided first to set aside some land for a cemetery and then to erect a church alongside the burial ground. At the end of May, Archdeacon Burd arrived to install Richard as 'Permanent Resident Minister'. This was the title he used on the cover of the Parish Magazine he soon produced to describe events taking place in the area, which was a territory covering (so Richard said) some 2,000 square miles. It included settlements at Fort Pitt, Frenchman Butte, River Junction (Deer Creek), Paradise Hill, Big Hill, White Eagle, Red Cross and Perch Lake. To cover this enormous territory Richard was provided with a car. It frequently broke down, sometimes shedding a wheel, developing a puncture, overheating or getting bogged down in the mud of the prairie trails. (Many years later Margaret recalled how she used to drive in Canada, which was something she wisely never attempted in England, because to have done so would have added chauffeur to her many other roles. We children would tease her by commenting, "It's easy to drive in Canada where the roads are as wide as the prairies!") But at least the Bishop was generous enough on one occasion to give him $50 towards its cost, while the archdeacon recommended that he should take no more than four services on a Sunday.

By June Richard was able to report in his Parish Magazine that work on the church at Fort Pitt had commenced and that land had been given for another church and cemetery at River Junction/Deer Creek. Letters of support and gifts were already arriving from many different sources – including Richard's friends and supporters in England, among them the Bishop of Sheffield and the Dean of Durham. Work on the church continued throughout the summer, interrupted only when 'operations were suspended until after threshing'. Richard's contribution to the work included nailing wooden shingles to the spire, added, as we have noticed already, on top of the church for Daisy Pepper's benefit. Money was scarce - 1929 was the year of the Wall Street crash - but articles and gifts in kind came from all members of the community: an altar, a bishop's chair, a cross and reading desk, brass vases and pews (made by a local carpenter). Throughout his life Richard was never afraid to ask for help. But it all came at some cost to his health, which was never robust at any time. In September the local doctor warned him that he was working too hard. This drew from Richard a typical response in the Parish Magazine, when he advertised that 'half a bottle of a particularly obnoxious tonic, free of charge, can be obtained upon application to the Church Farm, Fort Pitt. Owner has no further use for same!' It may well have been that a return, in the Fall, to Bishop's College, to continue with his studies came none too early. In October the archdeacon made another visit, this time accompanied by Bishop Lloyd. The church, though not complete, was ready for the first service, and a congregation of over 160 was present for its formal dedication.

By early February 1930 he was back again in Fort Pitt, though not without difficulty and some danger to his life. The first number of the Parish Magazine for that year contains this apology:

> 'I was very sorry to disappoint my good supporters at North Wingfield (Fort Pitt North) the other Sunday night when I got lost in the snow. I want to thank Kelly McClure for coming out on horseback to see me. He found me, minus horses and sleigh, in the deep snow, where I must have looked like one of the "Babes in the Wood". Like the Good Samaritan he put me on his own horse and brought me safely back to Fort Pitt, where we found that my team had made their way home and were standing against the stable door awaiting admittance. This is the third time I had got lost since the snow came. In a previous issue of the Magazine I made the statement that I was 98% Canadian. Since getting lost I am bound to amend this. I am now only 50% Canadian. Will John Mapletoft, Fred Pepper and C. Bairstow Rothery please note'

In the same magazine, at the ripe age of 27, he was bold enough to write:

> 'I would like it to be generally known that I shall use every means within my power to oppose the attempted introduction of Sunday picture shows or dances . . We can make Sunday a day of rest without a picture show or dance'.

> 'I wish to say that if I come across any instance where "moonshine" has been sold or given to a young lad or boy, I shall report it'.

References to the Peppers continued to increase. By now, it would seem that Richard had been accepted as part of the Pepper family. Fred and his sons provided practical help, in addition to rescuing him from the snow from time to time, and companionship. On one occasion Fred even lent him the family car when Richard's had shed a wheel which carried on of its own volition down the rutted prairie trail, as he recalled with glee many years later. With John, one of the triplets, he went camping down by the Saskatchewan River near the site of the old Hudson's Bay Company Post at Fort Pitt. There were continued outbreaks of measles and in such emergencies, or when other medical attention was required, Daisy Pepper was always a useful ally. Soon she became president of the Church Women's Association and we can be sure that she was always ready to provide a friendly welcome for a homesick Englishman. The Parish Magazine for February 1930 records that 'Miss Peggy Pepper has made an efficient sacristan at All Saints Church. We hope to retain her services for the coming year'. As indeed Richard did! This was a task Peggy continued to do, with great devotion, for the next 40 years.

During 1930 gifts and furnishings for the church continued to pour in - $5 for the cost of a much-needed extra stove, a pulpit bible, a portable organ, books for the minister's reference library, boxes of clothing, toys, food and games; even 'two lovely brass candlesticks, from Professor and Frau Wilmers of Mullhausen University, Germany, modelled from those in Nuremberg Cathedral, in memory of their daughter, Lottie (Mrs Kloecks), who was laid to rest in the new cemetery of All Saints'. By insisting, quite rightly, on continuing to use these candlesticks on the altar of the church, Richard was to fall foul of the 'protestant' church authorities, in the person of the new archdeacon who (in 1932) said to Richard "Take those candlesticks off the altar". "No, I will not", replied Richard, acutely aware of their precious significance.

This obstinacy and firmness in his convictions was both Richard's strength and his Achilles heel. Confrontations with or even a disregard of authority were characteristic of his life, originating perhaps in plain, north-country cussedness. He had had to struggle against his father when he decided to seek ordination and because he had not been to university he had been rejected by the church authorities in England. When he sought a future for himself in Canada, he found himself criticised because of his high church practices, which included a love of beauty and dignity in worship. It is not surprising that a perceptive Bishop of Salisbury said of him many years later, "There's a great deal of pain there".[19]

Perhaps it is fair to say that without his sense of inner conviction, without this obstinacy, Richard would not have made his way to north Saskatchewan in the first place, nor could he have survived the awful isolation and loneliness. Margaret has recollected how, during those early years, when she was sacristan at All Saints church, there were many occasions when "tears were shed in the vestry".

Alongside the struggles with authority and the continued appeals for help and money, there were lighter moments recalled in early photographs: 'with the boys at St. Walburg', 'shooting down by the river', puffing a pipe with 'old chief Waskassen' and a band of visiting Indians, or helping Fred Pepper, with several of 'Margaret's great brothers', working with teams of horses on the construction of the new highway. Wonderful recollections of his ministry were published later which provide a perceptive insight into the nature of his ministry and what life was like in those early settler communities.

> *'Preacher Taylor looked after christenings, deaths, marriages, even drunks and cattle-stealing at times. Someone sent him to see me. He explained that he wanted a church. Well, he said that if he got a church there would be a cemetery. I told him that I thought we could swing it, as I believed everyone would give either work or material. He got donations from Eatons, Simpsons, and God knows who else.*
>
> *He used to call on us once in a while and if anyone was sick he would pray for them. One day, in my unholy way, I told him, "Now look, no one is so sick and helpless that he can't ask God for help himself, but he probably can't get wood in or throw feed or water his stock. You think it over". He did: I guess he turned out to be a real help. He married a local girl, went back to England and raised a family'.[20]*

Margaret Young writes of the birth of her first daughter in July 1930:

---

[19] In conversation with myself in 1967. W.T.

[20] FPH page 532, recollections of Bert Mills in 1955.

'I had planned to stay with (the midwife) for the delivery of my eldest daughter. Joe (my husband) had left early that morning for St. Walburg, so I was alone, had done a few chores and mixed bread by 10 a.m. I had to lie down. When the baby was born I tied the cord with tape, wrapped a diaper around her and tucked her in bed beside me. In the meantime some little pigs pushed the kitchen door open and ate the boiled barley in the wash boiler by the door. A few hours later Mr Gaul stopped in with mail. When he heard what had happened, he rode and got Mrs Amirault (the midwife), who took care of us and baked the bread, then stayed until Joe came home in the evening. Three days later our minister, Dick Taylor, called for a visit. He asked if I would like to have the baby christened. I did not know of this christening, so after much discussion, it was done. When Joe came in for supper he had a newly baptised daughter'[21].

On the 5th October 1930 the churchyard at Fort Pitt was consecrated. On the same day Peggy was confirmed, with her sisters Rose and Mildred. Ten days later Peggy, or Margaret, as she came to be called by Richard, celebrated her 19th birthday and by the end of the year, when Richard had to return to Bishop's College for his final period of study, they had become engaged.

Events thereafter proceeded quickly. Richard continued with his studies and, at the same time his ministry at Fort Pitt and the surrounding area, as the following programme of services for Easter indicates. Because he was still a layman, an ordained clergyman, such as the archdeacon, had to be invited to the parish to celebrate services of Holy Communion.

EASTER SUNDAY April 5th 1931
11 a.m.　　　　　River Junction School (Deer Creek)
3 p.m.　　　　　All Saints Church Fort Pitt. Preacher: Richard M. Taylor

---

[21] FPH page 726.

EASTER WEDNESDAY   April 8th (weather and roads permitting)

11 a.m.   Holy   Communion   and   Sermon   at Paradise Hill

3 p.m.   Holy Communion and Sermon at Deer Creek

7.30 p.m.   Holy Communion and Sermon at Fort Pitt

(Preacher and Celebrant The Ven. W. Paul, Archdeacon of Saskatchewan).[22]

Indeed the archdeacon, with Mrs Paul, stayed in the area over Easter, both of them preaching and taking services. One wonders what conversations took place between them and Richard and Margaret. In June 1931, Richard received a certificate from the Bishop of Saskatchewan recognising that he had completed 57 out of the 87 subjects necessary before he could be qualified academically for Priest's Orders. The tragedy is that soon afterwards he was refused ordination to the diaconate at Prince Albert Cathedral. The reasons for this are not entirely clear. Margaret sadly recalled later that Richard's 'Anglo-Catholic' or 'high church' practices were irreconcilable with the 'Protestant' or 'low church' ethos of the Diocese of Saskatchewan, which was engaged, throughout this time, in a fierce competition with the Roman Catholic missionaries for the 'souls' of the Indians. So it was as a layman that he was married to Margaret at All Saints Church on 17th August 1931. The ceremony was taken by Canon Cross from Lloydminster, Henry Ellis from Onion Lake and Bishop de Carteret of Jamaica (on furlough from his diocese which he had generously volunteered to spend in the missionary diocese of Saskatchewan).[23] Richard's best man was one of the triplets, Charles Pepper, while Margaret's bridesmaid was her sister, Mildred.

Some 70 years later Margaret was persuaded to talk about the background to this occasion. The ceremony had to take place at

---

[22] It was Archdeacon Burd who had installed Richard as Minister-in-Charge (i.e. still a layman) in May 1929.

[23] Bishop de Carteret was a bachelor. One condition he placed on agreeing to officiate was that if, in due course, Richard and Margaret should have a son, he was to be named after him: hence the proliferation of my initials.
W. R. de C. M. T.

nine o'clock on a Monday morning because Bishop de Carteret was on his way, after staying at Onion Lake, to other engagements in the area. Fred was proud to give her away, calling her 'one of my chickens' (she was, after all, his first daughter by Daisy). There was little or no money, because Richard did not receive a regular stipend, and Margaret's wedding shoes, on mail order, failed to arrive in time. So, much to her chagrin, she had to borrow some black ones from her sister-in-law, Maud. They set off from Fort Pitt by car on their way to Edmonton, pausing first at Vermilion, where they met Grace, who was working as a cook with a construction gang. Her generous gift of $35 was most welcome. Along the way Margaret was able to appreciate, for the first time, the joys of running hot water. Then it was back to Fort Pitt in time for the next Sunday services. But with the boundless optimism and faith in each other, that was to be so characteristic of their life together, they set up home in the primitive parsonage next door to the Church. Not long afterwards they welcomed the clergy and wives of the Lloydminster Deanery Convention to Fort Pitt, as was recorded in the Saskatchewan Diocesan Letter for 10th October 1931:

> 'The Lloydminster Deanery Convention was held in Fort Pitt on Tuesday and Wednesday, September 15th and 16th 1931. The roads and ferry approaches were in terrible shape and during most of the time it rained incessantly. The difficulties of the trip were soon forgotten by the smiling welcome and warm-hearted hospitality of Mr and Mrs R.M. Taylor and their band of willing W.A. workers. This is the first time a gathering of this nature has been held in historic Fort Pitt. Two years ago the Church owned nothing in the district. Today there is a beautiful Church and Parsonage and three acres of land nicely fenced. All the delegates were loud in their praises of the initiative and energy of Mr Taylor and his parishioners. Here is a complete answer to anybody who may question the worth of missions'.

Soon after this weather conditions made travel even more difficult, so Richard and Margaret settled down to face together the full rigours of a Saskatchewan winter in the primitive timber-frame parsonage that had been built near the church at Fort Pitt. The future that lay ahead of them was bleak. But news of Richard's enthusiastic church-building activities, and of his uncompromising churchmanship, must have filtered east to the Diocese of Algoma in Ontario, where the ecclesiastical authorities were more sympathetic to such attitudes. Early in 1932 the Bishop of Algoma invited Richard to move to the Manitoulin Island in Lake Huron, but it was with a heavy heart that Margaret said goodbye, in February 1932, to her home and family. She never saw her father again (he died in 1941). She, at the age of 20, and Richard were driven by Charlie in a sleigh-wagon over the frozen north Saskatchewan River to Lloydminster, where they caught the train to Saskatoon, Winnipeg and the east.

8 Mindemoya. 1932 - 36.

A look at the map will show that, by journeying east from Saskatchewan to Ontario, Richard and Margaret retraced the route taken by the early settlers as Canada was opened up to them. The railway had come to Frenchman Butte in 1928, just a few months before Richard first arrived in Saskatchewan. Now they used it to travel from Lloydminster to Little Current on the Manitoulin Island. Situated in the northern part of Lake Huron, this island straddled the waterborne route used by the early explorers, voyageurs, traders and missionaries. By a happy coincidence they found themselves in one of the most sacred places in North America. A recent book on the subject describes:

> 'the story of Manitoulin's creation (is) rich in sacred significance. Based on translations from the Ojibway, Odawa (Ottawa) and Potawatomi languages, Manitou means 'spirit', or 'the Great Spirit'. The island is also known as Gitchi Manitou, Manitoulin or Manitouminiss, meaning 'Isle of the Manitou', or 'Spirit Island'. Gitichi Manitou had a dream, a vision of all that is good, and a mandate to fulfil his dream. He began by making the four elements – fire, earth, water and wind. From these he created humans and bestowed on them the greatest gift of all – the ability to dream[24].

The name Mindemoya refers particularly to the island in the middle of the lake with the same name. In my childhood Richard used to delight in telling us the legends connected with that name, because the island is supposed to resemble an old woman on her hands and knees. According to the legend:

> Kitche Manitou (the Great Spirit), creator of the Universe, sent Nanabush, the son of a human mother and spirit father, to teach the Anishnaabeg (i.e. those who live on the Manitoulin). Nanabush, who was raised by his grandmother, possessed supernatural powers, including the power of transformation. According to one legend, Nanabush was running from the south, with his grandmother over his

---

[24] *Sacred Places in North America.* Courtney Milne. p. 19.

shoulder. She was heavy, but he got as far as Mindemoya when he stumbled and lost his balance. His grandmother flew through the air, landing on her hands and knees in the middle of the lake, where she remains.[25]

There is however no evidence that Richard ever did any work with the Indians, or 'native persons', whose language, faith and culture is such an integral part of the early history of the Manitoulin. When the bishop in his letter to Richard said that 'the people of Mindemoya on the Manitoulin Island have petitioned me to send them a missionary', he almost certainly had just the need of the first settlers on his mind. These folk, for the most part, were of European origin: the Anglican church that was soon to be erected, in response to Richard's enthusiasm and vision, reflected those origins, with its extraordinary collection of artefacts, stones, statues and furnishings, collected by-and-large from England. The final structure was a triumphant statement of English Anglicanism. It is none the worse for that.

It is interesting to set the legends of Mindemoya within the wider context of the situation and history of the Manitoulin Island. The largest fresh-water island in the world, it is a beautiful place. About 80 miles long from east to west, it varies in width (north to south) from two to thirty miles. It is itself sprinkled with more than 80 lakes, one of the largest of which is Lake Mindemoya. There are two ways of approaching the island. The first, used by Richard and Margaret in 1932, is from the north, using a branch of the railway on to the island at Little Current. Nowadays one drives south from the Trans-Canada Highway through Espanola or approaches from the south, by driving up the Bruce Peninsula from Toronto and then crossing over from Tobermory on the ferry to South Baymouth.

Lakes, limestone, pastureland, maple trees, abundant fishing, wildlife, berries,[26] these are some of the features that still attract sportsmen and settlers to the island. It has an unspoilt beauty that echoes the magic of its name. This territory was occupied when the Europeans arrived at the end of the 15th century.

---

[25] *Exploring Manitoulin.* Shelley J. Pearen. p. 157.

[26] It is believed that early pioneers were once saved from starvation by eating the berries off the hawthorn tree. Today the term "Haw Eater" signifies someone born on Manitoulin. Pearen p. 35.

THE RIVER GOES ON

Among these native people were the Iroquois, who relied mainly on agriculture, and the Algonquins, who survived by fishing and hunting. The latter included the Ojibwa, who make up most of Manitoulin's native population today.

The arrival of Europeans had an enormous effect on all the natives. Natives provided the Europeans with survival skills and furs: Europeans provided the natives with cloth, tools, and weapons which, eventually, drastically altered their lives and traditions. When the French explorer, Samuel de Champlain, arrived in 1603, he encountered Algonquins and their Iroquois allies. . . . In addition to explorers and fur traders, France sent Roman Catholic missionaries. Champlain's aim was to establish a colony and to Christianize the natives, as well as to develop a system of trading posts. To implement his ideas, Champlain sent for Jesuit missionaries . . They lived among the natives, established missions, and learned their language in order to convert them to Christianity. . . In 1648 Jesuit missionary Father Joseph Poncet was sent to the Manitoulin to establish a mission for Algonquian-speaking natives. He was the first European resident of 'Ile-de-Ste-Marie'.

Unfortunately those eager European missionaries and traders spread not only the gospel and trade, but European diseases. Experts have estimated that there were about one million natives in Canada in 1500 and by 1600 their population had shrunk by 90 per cent. The original migration of the native people via the Arctic had provided a disease barrier through extreme climate, and, until the arrival of the Europeans, they had been sheltered from these diseases.

In 1630 raiding Iroquois caused Father Poncet to abandon the Manitoulin Island mission . . Following the Iroquois raids the island appears to have been visited only sporadically by natives on fishing and hunting expeditions until the next permanent mission was established at Wikwemikong on the east. . . To cleanse the island of contagious illness it was burned clean. It took a century or more for the vegetation and wildlife to return to their former state.[27]

---

[27] Pearen pp. 4,5.

In the 19th century both natives and settlers began to return to the island and a complex series of treaties and agreements attempted, with limited success, to encourage the natives to live in settlements. From 1830 to 1860 an 'Establishment' was organised on the island at Mantitowaning, consisting of a government-supported superintendent, doctor, carpenter, and various mechanics, and an Anglican-supported clergyman, all to instruct the natives in the 'ways of civilisation'. Thus the church at Manitowaning was the first Anglican church to be built in northern Ontario. It is now part of what is called 'Great Spirit Island Parish', which also includes Mindemoya and South Baymouth. The first Manitoulin land was offered for sale in June 1866, though enthusiastic settlers had already begun to arrive two years earlier. These early settlers typically arrived in small family groups. Most were of similar background and nationality: many were English, Irish or Scottish Protestants from the nearby counties of southern Ontario; people whose parents had emigrated from Great Britain a few decades earlier. Land was sold to them for fifty cents an acre, for cash, to a maximum of 200 acres. The new owner had to occupy the land within six months and could obtain a patent after residing for three years and clearing 10 of the 200 acres.

Against this background we are fortunate to have Richard's own charming account, written of his arrival with Margaret on the Manitoulin Island in 1932 and the building of St. Francis of Assisi Church at Mindemoya. He begins with a letter from the bishop.

....

"ROCKSBOROUGH, by Divine Permission Lord Bishop of ALGOMA, [a vast Diocese extending north of the Great Lakes in Canada from Fort William almost down to Toronto], wrote to me out of the blue at the beginning of one of the years of the Great Depression before the last war. I was at Fort Pitt in northern Saskatchewan, where I had been sent four years before by the late Bishop Lloyd to open up a new Anglican mission amongst the settlers and Indians north of the north Saskatchewan River on the Alberta border. These folk and I had built several comely little wooden churches and a mission-house for my Canadian wife and me.

THE RIVER GOES ON

The bishop wrote: 'I have word of your work at Fort Pitt and roundabout. The people of MINDEMOYA on the MANITOULIN ISLAND in LAKE HURON have petitioned me to send them a missionary. Will you go? Diocesan funds are at a very low ebb and I fear I can offer you no stipend'. We were deposited in the darkness and the snow of a very cold late-winter afternoon at the northern tip of Manitoulin Island with our luggage and one dollar and a few cents in Canadian currency. We were told that a man with a team of horses and a sleigh would shortly be leaving with His Majesty's Mails for the thirty-five-mile journey to Mindemoya in the heart of the island. The price for the journey would be two dollars and two bits each (two bits = 25 cents), with the luggage thrown in. This sportsman agreed to take a chance and let us owe the money to him. Whereupon, without ado, we made ourselves comfortable on the bags of His Majesty's Mails on the back of the sleigh and set off into the crisp darkness.

Most of the male inhabitants of Mindemoya were lounging around the red-hot pot-bellied stove in Mr A.J. Wagg's Post-Office-cum-Store that night. It was not a reception committee for the two rather stiff and cold young folk who had arrived in their midst, but a group of men who had spent some sociable hours together awaiting the weekly arrival of the mail and its renewal of their visible link with the outside world and its events. Not, I say, a reception committee, for Diocesan H.Q. had forgotten to tell the good folk of Mindemoya that we were coming. There was then no hotel in the place and we were tired and hungry. Like that of Abou Ben Adhem (may his tribe increase!), the name of Mr Chauncey Berry led all the rest of the signatories to the petition which had put about two thousand miles between us and Fort Pitt. He was a widower and lived alone, so I gathered, in a partly furnished frame house about half a mile out of the settlement, where he operated a saw and planing mill. I left my young wife beside the stove in the store and went out in search of Mr Berry. He had retired for the night, but, after I had told him of my errand, got up in good Christian fashion, heaped an armful of logs into the stove and told me to fetch Margaret from the store.

We lived with him for some months. I worked part-time in his saw and planing mill and my wife did the housekeeping in return for our board and lodging.

The following morning we collected our gear from the store and set about posting notices announcing that an

Anglican church service would be held in the school the following Sunday at 3 p.m. Meanwhile Chauncey Berry and I made a rough wooden altar table and a cross to place upon it, while Margaret produced a pair of domestic candlesticks and candles from our trunk. The school was packed to the doors for this first Church of England service ever to be held in the community. The congregation was without hymnbooks or prayer books, but I played well-known hymns on the school piano, saying each verse before we sang it, and we did very well. Unfortunately there were no churchwardens as yet, or sidesmen, and consequently no collection – which was a pity for we could have used a few dollars to great advantage. (It didn't happen again!). In the evenings during the following weeks we had marvellous meetings in the farmhouses and homes of the settlers. Everyone came, men, women and children. I would talk about religion and the Church and its history. Later the womenfolk provided refreshments (a 'lunch' it was always called) and we talked and talked and I answered questions.

By-and-by we thought that it would be a good idea to build a little church of our own. The school was all very well for services, but it was also used for community dances and affairs on Saturday evenings and the French chalk and chewing gum on the floor were a bit putting-off. I prepared some plans for a log church and we were given a splendid site in the middle of Mindemoya. Then the owner of a large saw-mill on Lake Manitowaning, which was the largest of more than 100 lakes on the island told us that if we cared to haul the logs to his mill we could have the free use of it to convert our logs into framing, floor joists, spars, rafters and boarding. I drew some fresh and more ambitious plans for a frame church. So it was until one evening, at a house meeting, I was talking about St. Francis of Assisi and of how he carried stones into the wood to repair the little church. The Manitoulin Island is 80 miles long and 30 miles wide in its widest part. What isn't pre-Cambrian shield is splendid hard limestone. We would be latter-day followers of Blessed Francis and build a lovely stone Church ourselves! More plans. Splendid plans! We formed ourselves into groups. One group to go into the bush and cut down an enormous number of great maple and pine trees. Another group to quarry the stone. Another group to clear the site of sixteen-feet-deep of beautiful sand and gravel down to a perfectly flat stone table, smoothed and scored by the passage of ice at the close of some infinitely remote ice age. ***Upon a rock I will build my church!*** All through the following winter, trees and stone were hauled across the snow and ice - the trees to the mill and seven hundred loads of stone to the site of the church. Some of us worked in Chauncey Berry's mill, making doors and window frames. Later, some more men made lime-kilns and burnt great quantities of lime for the mortar to mix with the gravel and sand which Divine Providence had deposited on the church plot an aeon before in readiness for the building of His House.

We quarried most of our stone from a great escarpment of limestone well inland. We needed lots of dynamite. The Ontario Government Highways Department offered to give us dynamite, caps, fuse-wire and drills, and we borrowed an old model T Ford and crossed over to the mainland and over the mountains to Espanola to collect it. We of the dynamite party are likely always to remember the hazardous journey back over the rough roads with such a sensitive load.

We drilled a series of holes four feet deep and four yards apart along fifty yards at the top of the escarpment. One of my less attractive duties was to hold erect a great steel drill and turn it around at intervals whilst a great strong man smote the top of it with an enormous sledgehammer. This task took some weeks of real labour. We then inserted sticks of dynamite into the holes and connected the whole lot with fuse wire. The end of the fuse-train was lit and all ran like hell out of the way. The enormous explosion which followed shook the whole island, but there, at the bottom of the escarpment was lovely, lovely limestone, ready to be moved away.

So far we had spent no money for we hadn't any, but we needed cement, new belts for the saw-and-planing-mills, more tools, nails, roofing, glass and a hundred other things. I determined to go down into eastern Canada to the cities on a begging expedition. It was to be "an act of faith". I wrote to Rocksborough, our bishop. This produced his reluctant permission to go, with a solemn warning not to expect him to come and 'bail me out' if I ran into trouble. He detailed one of the Cowley Fathers from Bracebridge to come and take charge of my parish in my absence. Enough money was scraped together to pay for a one-way ticket on the railway to Toronto. Standing alone on the platform of the huge station in Toronto at eight o'clock the following morning, very conscious of not knowing a single soul in that great city, some of my fine enthusiasm began to evaporate. Certainly "one step enough for me", but where the step? Suddenly I thought that a city like Toronto would have a Toc H mark or hostel? Sure enough – there it was in the telephone directory – Toc H. Mark 11C, 614 Huron Street. Jim Newton, the warden, who answered the telephone, quite sure that he had to deal with some young lunatic Englishman, nobly rose to the occasion. "Come on right up and you will be in time for breakfast". I said that I had no money to pay for my transportation. "Hang on then", he said, "and one of the boys will come and get you". The Toc H Mark family was eighteen young men: medical students from the Banting Institute, men reading at the University, one or two young stockbrokers and law students. Over breakfast I told them about the building of St. Francis of Assisi at Mindemoya. They formed themselves into a supporting committee. I was to stay at the Mark as their guest as long as maybe. One of the stockbrokers lent me his spare Dodge motor-car and furnished me with a credit card for free gas at the city gas stations and in the exciting days and nights which followed I bent myself to my task.

The president of the Canada Cement Corporation (when, after a little persistence with doorkeepers and secretaries, I gained his presence) told me that he admired my damned cheek in forcing my way into his office. He not only gave me 100 bags of Portland cement, but agreed to have it shipped free from Toronto up the Great Lakes to the Manitoulin Island. The president of the Dunlop Rubber Company furnished me with great rolls of assorted driving-belts for our saw-and-planing-mills. The President of the Canadian Bank of Commerce took me out to luncheon and introduced me to some influential friends who caught the church-building bug as a result. The president of the Canadian Wrought Iron and Copper Company was somewhat less enthusiastic when I called on him. He invited me to step down out of the clouds and added, "We are going through a great depression and my firm is finding it difficult to keep our men in employment". I said that I thought it was a godly and a Christian notion to keep men from the bread lines and why didn't we have a little prayer and ask God to help. And so we did, right in his office as we knelt together on the floor by his desk. He then took me into his drawing-office and introduced me to some of the staff. I sketched out on a drawing board a rough design for a great Altar Cross, to be cast in a new gold-like alloy, and outlines and measurements of the wrought-iron strap-hinges for the church doors. These they promised to make for us to the greater glory of God. [Some months later I returned to Toronto to collect the cross and the door-hinges. President Lee took me into the showrooms and with great pride showed me the lovely cross. He said that the men had made it in their own time – draughtsmen, pattern makers, foundry-men, polishers and buffers. "We've been mighty proud to make it", he said. "A few days after you left we were awarded the contract to make all the copper doors, grills, windows and fittings of the great new skyscraper bank now being built. We never looked back!" They added to their princely gifts a pair of wonderful Swedish wrought-iron lamps for the church entrance.] The Canadian Pacific Railway had just completed the Royal York Hotel in downtown Toronto – a vast skyscraper and then the largest hotel in the British Empire. There I addressed a luncheon gathering of businessmen and spoke about the church and St. Francis. Afterwards I wrote to Sir Edward Beattie, the president of the C.P.R., and congratulated him on his fine hotel. I said that I particularly admired the acres of lovely carpets and how nice it would be if some could be found for the greater glory of God and his little Church then a-building at Mindemoya. He replied personally and kindly and asked me to tell him about sizes and colours. He had some especially made, in beautiful greens, five feet wide, to fit down the church aisle all the way from the Altar to the West End. He added to his gift a carpet for the vestry and one for the Mission House, when it should be built. The president of the company making hot-air heating furnaces was less sure about giving me a furnace to warm the church in winter. 'In any case', he said, 'I am not sure I am in complete sympathy with the Anglican Church'. I told him that when he eventually arrived at the gate of Heaven he would find it very awkward having to explain to St. Peter (not to say St. Francis as well) that he had refused so great an opportunity to help God's children at Mindemoya. He saw the point and the magnificent heating arrangements (now, I am told, converted to oil burning), so long enjoyed by the company of the faithful at Mindemoya, have been a lasting testimony to the warmth inside many an apparently cold human exterior.

So it was that I arrived back on the island with nearly two thousand dollars and, for many weeks afterwards, cement, roofing-tiles, crates of glass, kegs of nails, rolls of insulation and the like, came pouring in – to say nothing of carpets and many more kind letters and donations. 'So we built the wall, for the people had a mind to work', as Nehemiah had said so many years before.

In the summer, tourists from the U.S.A. find their way up to the Manitoulin Island. It was so that church-building summer. One afternoon, inside a pair of limey overalls, I was busy below mixing mortar for the builders up on the outside of the rapidly-rising walls of the church, when a rich-looking American pulled up and got out of his car and walked over to me. 'Say', he said, 'this is a mighty-fine Church to be building up here in the backwoods. More suitable for a city'. I explained, with gentleness, that we were doing it for the glory of God. 'How', he asked, 'are you raising the money in these hard times?' I replied, 'Well it's like this. All the men you see here are giving their labour, which is all they have to give. Every time someone drives up in a fine car and asks your sort of question, I ask him for a donation.' He peeled fifty dollars from a great roll of bills and went thoughtfully on his way, assured of our prayers for himself, and his household. Frank Scott Clarke, from Detroit, the great American artist of his day, would not make me a definite promise to do a great altarpiece for us. It was not in his line, he said. When he came back to the Island the following year he sent his chauffeur in a fine car to take me down at once to a large summer lodge on the edge of the lake, where he was entertaining Big Bill Thompson, the mayor of Chicago, and other notabilities. Frank looked rather frail, I thought, as he welcomed me, and introduced me around. He told me that he had been very ill in Detroit during the winter and his life had been despaired of. One day, as he lay in his great four-poster bed, he saw a perfect vision of Christ in His Agony in the Garden of Gethsemane. He rang his bell and summoned his wife and nurse and said, "I've got to get better, for I must paint the picture I have seen for the young priest at Mindemoya". Soon he was strong enough to be wheeled into his studio. There, on a great piece of specially ordered Belgian canvas – the exact width of the space between the bed-posts of his bed – he began the splendid Altarpiece which his manservant later unrolled for me on the floor of his summer lodge. Mrs Scott Clarke had brought up from New Orleans a magnificent pair of Louis X1V Altar candlesticks to complete the furnishing of the Altar. 'A thank-offering', she said, 'for Frank's miraculous recovery'.

The Right Honourable R.B. Bennett, Prime Minister of Canada (later Lord Bennett), together with the Premier of Ontario and his entire Cabinet, produced the money which paid for the shipping of pieces of stone from Canterbury Cathedral, York Minster, St. Paul's Cathedral, Glastonbury, Fountains Abbey and Lincoln Cathedral. These were built into the sanctuary walls and marked with bronze plaques, giving details of origin and donors. Sir Henry Thornton, the president of Canadian National Railways, gave and sent to us a bell from a fine old trans-Canada locomotive. This bell, after much journeying to and fro across Canada, now hangs in the Tower and summons the faithful to a more splendid adventure.

The church stands fair and square with a huge tower. Two storeys all above ground level. The first floor [i.e. the ground floor] is the church hall for Sunday School and parish do's and corporate breakfasts after Sunday Communion, with a beautifully-equipped kitchen, furnished with dishes bearing the badge of St. Francis – a gift from the potteries of Langton in Staffordshire. These and a fine cook-stove (which is another story!). Upstairs is the church proper – the very holy and lovely place, with a flickering-swinging light marking the Presence. Riddel hangings at the altar, embroidered by the Ladies of Honour of the Court of Elizabeth 1, flanking Scott's great 'Agony' and Frontals which once graved the High Altar of Salisbury Cathedral.

'And the people are glad to go up into the House of the Lord: they and their children. For ever and ever. Amen'.

....

It was perhaps fortunate that those 'two rather stiff and cold young folk', who arrived unexpectedly in Wagg's Post-Office-cum-Store that cold night in February 1932, had little idea what lay ahead of them. Otherwise they might have turned back. But they had no choice. Richard had 'burnt his boats' as far as the Diocese of Saskatchewan was concerned and they had no money. Nor was any forthcoming in the immediate future from the Diocese of Algoma, whose bishop, Rocksborough Smith, or 'Rocky', as he was usually referred to behind his back, had not had the courtesy to warn the good folk of Mindemoya that Richard and Margaret were on their way. They were young. Richard had just celebrated his 29th birthday, Margaret was not yet 21. He was driven by a strong sense of calling and a determination to get ordained; she was utterly devoted to him, even to the extent of almost entirely subsuming her own identity, for the rest of his life, in that of her husband. So they settled down to life in Mindemoya, living first with Chauncey Berry, before moving to a tiny uninsulated wooden house down by Lake Mindemoya. That first winter on the island was bitterly cold. It might seem surprising, after Margaret had grown up in freezing Saskatchewan, but at Fort Pitt their house was at least insulated. Not so on the Manitoulin, where the first to wake in the morning had to get up to relight the stove or stoke the wood burner and then jump rapidly back under the bedclothes.

Richard was not therefore a 'missionary' in the usual sense of the word, though the Diocese of Algoma, at that time, was described as a missionary diocese, because it was not financially independent and relied, to a large extent, for its survival on subventions from 'the old country'. Four years later and from 1936 to 1938, as we shall see, Richard was asked to devote himself entirely to a campaign to establish an endowment fund that would enable the diocese to be independent.

Money, or the lack of it, was a factor which loomed large in the lives of everyone during the early anxious years of the 1930s. Unemployment was rife; indeed the fact that so many men were unemployed meant that they were free to work on St. Francis church, as Richard himself describes so well. His own financial position was precarious (as it was throughout his life). Many years later Margaret recalled how grateful they were to receive a gift from 'the old country' which came in the form of a parcel from Queen Mary's Guild. This included clothing for the children, a musquash coat for herself, and various household essentials. Meanwhile, Richard had the good sense to make good friends with the local bank manager, Jim Burt, who became one of his churchwardens and, in due course, my godfather. The other churchwarden, another William Taylor, later became part of the family when his son, Dennis, married Margaret's sister, Mildred. (As she said to us, 70 years later, "I came to Mindemoya to visit my sister and fell madly in love".)

For the three consecutive years, 1933, '34 and '35, that Richard was 'minister-in-charge' at Mindemoya, he had to make statistical returns to the Diocese of Algoma. These have survived. They make poignant reading. In 1933 his net stipend was $570.25, of which $261.92 came from the parish and $308.33 from the Synod Office. In that year the Women's Association bought a cook-stove for the parsonage and one wonders how they managed beforehand. In 1934 his stipend increased to $606.68: it included a Christmas offering of $7.50 from the congregation, but $12 per month had to be paid in rent for the parsonage. For 1935 the situation improved: his net salary was $690.73. During this time the total population of Mindemoya, Providence Bay and Big Lake – the three settlements for which Richard was responsible – gradually increased from 500 to 560 people, about 200 of whom were nominally Anglican. Services taken averaged about three per week. In 1933 there were three baptisms, one of which was mine. In 1934 there were two, one of which was that of my sister, Elizabeth. In 1935, by which time Richard was in deacon's orders, there was a confirmation service which necessarily implied a visit of the bishop to the parish.

We need to remind ourselves that throughout these heroic years, during which Richard was the driving-force behind the construction of St. Francis church, he was still not ordained. A photograph of the synod of the Diocese of Algoma, taken at Sault Ste. Marie in June 1932, shows him standing in sad and lonely isolation at one end of the back row, conspicuous in collar and tie among serried ranks of deep dog-collared clergy.

Throughout that first year at Mindemoya (1932), Richard and Margaret changed home with some frequency. From their initial lodgings with Chauncey Berry, they moved north down to the primitive house by Lake Mindemoya, on what is now charmingly called 'Ketchankooken Drive'. Later they moved back up to Main Street, to a bungalow where in 1933 I was born; then to a flat above Bond's hardware store, where in 1934 Elizabeth was born. Both houses were still there in 2002. Main Street, which runs

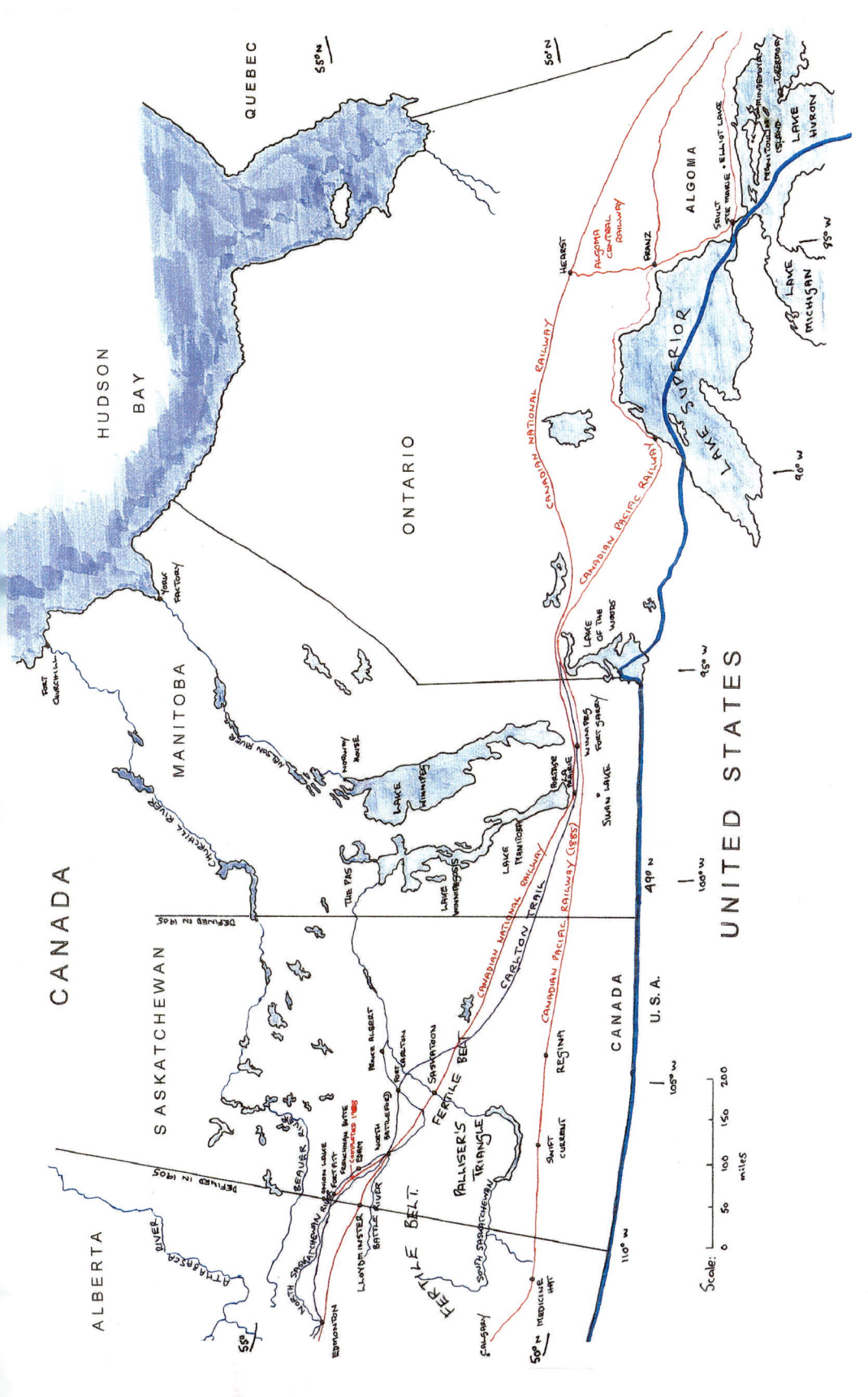

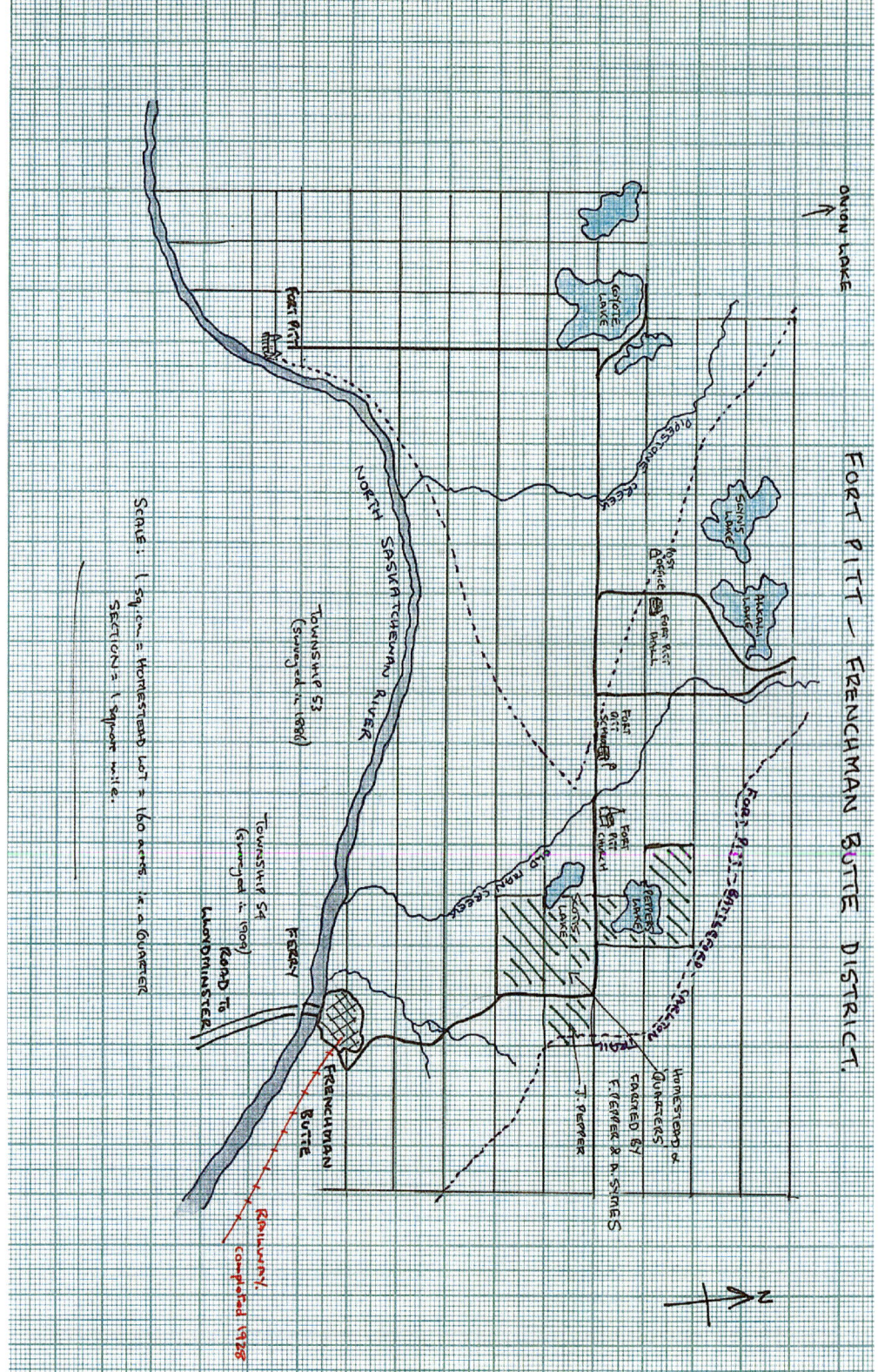

URANIUM MINES

St. FRANCIS' CHURCH

MANITOULIN ISLAND
ONTARIO, CANADA

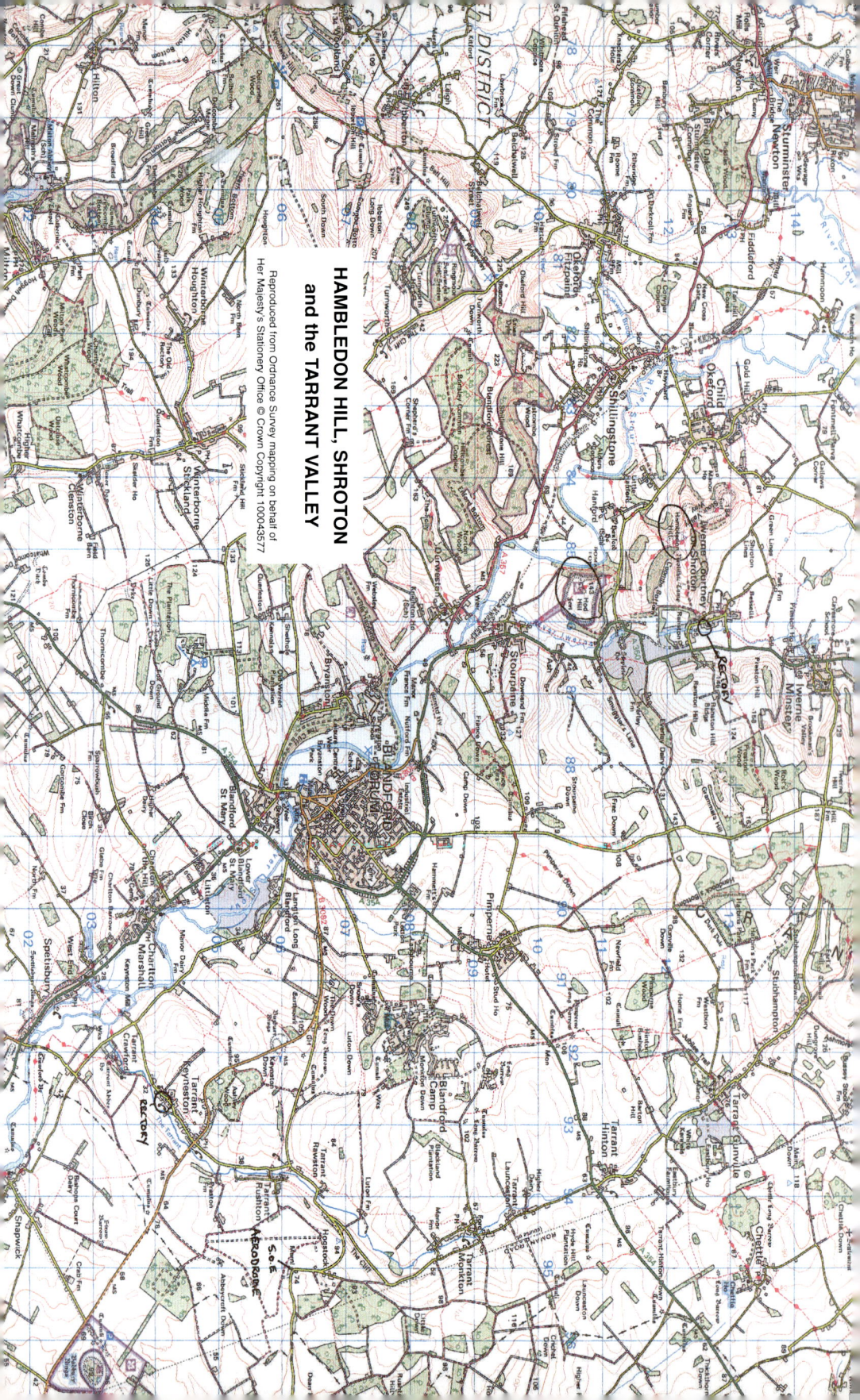

HAMBLEDON HILL, SHROTON
and the TARRANT VALLEY

east and west, has been tidied up over the years. It is no longer a dirt road. Wagg's Store has, for many years, been the main dairy cum creamery on the island. Churchwarden Jim Burt's Bank of Montreal is now a modern brick building. Out on the west is the Church of St. Francis, one of the landmarks of the Manitoulin Island, lovingly cherished and now with a fine extension on the eastern end, completed in 2001, which gives easy access for coffins and wheelchairs.

Life for Margaret was lonely, as indeed it was for most women in that isolated community. She had few friends. All provisions came from Wagg's store and for most of her time she was preoccupied with domestic work – making bread, preparing meals and looking after her young children. In this she had some help from local girls, two of whom, Norah Smith and Frances Cox, were still alive in 2002 and remembered her fondly. When I was born she was alone in the house while Richard went off at 5 p.m., as it was getting dark, to help in hauling logs across the ice to the sawmill. By the time he returned home at 7p.m., the midwife, Mary Brown had arrived, and so had I – safely installed in the bottom drawer of a chest of drawers, because there was no cot. When my sister Elizabeth arrived 19 months later, Margaret was again busy, at 12.30 p.m., making apple pies for a gang of six men from the building project. By 2 p.m. the baby had arrived and, one presumes, that lunch was ready.

The fact that Richard was still a layman until December 1934 did not hinder his extraordinary efforts at creating an Anglican Christian community in the centre of Manitoulin Island. The registers of the church show that the first Anglican service to be held in Mindemoya was Evensong on April 10th, 1932, when no less that 120 people crowded into the hall. A month later, on May 8th, 70 people came to a service in Providence Bay. Later that year, on Sunday July 17th, Bishop Rocksborough Smith made his first visit to the 'Mindemoya Mission', when 230 folk turned out to welcome him for Evensong. These bare statistics are evidence of the support that Richard was receiving for his determination to build something unique on the island – not just a community, but a stone church in which it could worship. Hence the laying of the foundation stone by Archdeacon Balfour, on June 15th, was a highly significant occasion.

1933 was a significant year in other ways. At the end of January, just a few weeks before I was born on March 20th, Adolf Hitler became Chancellor of Germany. It is unlikely that the news ever filtered through to the Manitoulin Island. There was no radio and, of course, no television; and the only newspaper, the Manitoulin Expositor, appeared but once a week. When it reached Mindemoya no doubt Richard and Margaret thought little of it. But in a profound way, the evil genius of Hitler, and all that he stood for, was to affect their lives, and that of their growing family, in ways that we shall discover in due course. Of more immediate concern was the birth of their first child, the work on the building of the church and, maybe, the news from the United States that the era of Prohibition had ended and, in November, that F.D. Roosevelt was elected president.

Next year, 1934, the work of church building continued, with the walls and tower completed and the roof timbers in place. That same year, on October 9th, my sister Elizabeth was born. Named after his beloved mother, she was always 'the apple of her father's eye'. In childhood she was known as Betty, but in the 1950s this was changed to Bess, the name we shall use from now on in this narrative. Two months later, on December 16th, Richard was made deacon in the cathedral at Sault Ste. Marie. It must have been a proud and precious moment for him. Almost six years to the day after leaving England for Canada, and after numerous vicissitudes, he could at last be called 'Reverend'. On the way he had built a church at Fort Pitt, fallen in love with and married Margaret and now they were the proud parents of a son and a daughter. No wonder we find, among his papers, a photograph of St. Francis' church, taken a month later in January 1935, complete by then with its roof, though there are no signs of a proper door, with the caption below, "God reigns: His Kingdom Come!" Finally Bishop Rocksborough Smith made a visit to Mindemoya to celebrate the first communion in the completed church on July 25th, followed by its dedication on Sunday August 1st 1935[28]. Perhaps it was on this

---

[28] The Church could not be consecrated until 21st June 1945, when it was free of all debt.

occasion that Richard invited the Bishop and others to come for a meal afterwards. So many people turned up that Margaret had to use a dustbin lid in which to make another apple pie. One wonders how she baked it.

Thereafter events moved swiftly. At long last, on December 15th 1935, Richard was ordained priest in the Cathedral. It was a proud moment on a cold day. A precious photograph of the clergy gathered for the occasion in the snow shows them grouped around the enigmatic figure of the Bishop, clad in all his episcopal glory in cope and mitre. The other clergy, though not Richard, wear a bizarre assortment of head-gear to protect themselves from the cold: one cleric is wearing a Homburg hat to go with his cassock and surplice; another that strange Anglican creation, a Canterbury cap, with its four corners pointing up to the sky.

Perhaps it was to celebrate his ordination, or just that a timely gift of $48 made it possible, Richard decided almost immediately afterwards to return to England for a brief holiday. He had been away from Derbyshire for seven long years, now he could return home, a priest at last, to introduce his young Canadian wife Margaret to his parents. By that time she was pregnant with their third child, Patricia. With them were myself, not quite three years old, and Bess, just sixteen months old. With him Richard carried a precious certificate issued by the bishop, acknowledging his good standing as a priest and authorising him to proceed to England on leave during February and March. This certificate is dated January 24th, 1936. In February the little family took passage, in the SS *Manchester Port*, which was a small cargo vessel that carried a few passengers, from Montreal to Manchester.

9 Derbyshire and Algoma 1936 – 38

When Richard and Margaret sailed from Montreal in February 1936 they had every expectation of returning to Canada a few months later. A brief note in the Algoma Missionary News for March/April 1936 reported: *"The Revd. R.M. and Mrs Taylor are enjoying a short vacation in England and are expected to return about the end of May."* But for Margaret that short vacation was to turn into a lifetime of exile from her homeland and her family. For Richard it was different. He was returning home, a priest at last. He could look forward to seeing his beloved mother and Derbyshire again. Maybe his father would be glad to see him, proud of the building-work he had achieved.

The journey across the Atlantic was a nightmare experience for Margaret. The weather was foul and for most of the crossing, which took 14 days, she was violently seasick. At times she must have been fearful for the health of the child she was carrying. In contrast Richard enjoyed the Atlantic voyage and so apparently did I, revelling in the rough weather in a manner I was not to repeat during my subsequent career in the Navy.

True to its name, the SS *Manchester Port* sailed past Liverpool and up the Ship Canal, to dock in Manchester, where the weary passengers were met by my grandfather William Taylor and taken to St. Laurence at North Wingfield in Derbyshire. There Margaret met the rest of the family for the first time: the always reassuring and gentle presence of my grandmother Elizabeth (or Nanny), and my aunt Dena with her husband John Mottershaw and their three children (all born while Richard was away in Canada): Gordon, the oldest grandchild, Anne, just two weeks older than me, and June, just a few months older than Bess. With the arrival of Pat, just a few months later in June 1936, we were in due course to become a lively group of cousins.

But even before Pat was born the little family was to be split up in what proved to be a terrible and harsh way. At this distance in time the exact details of what occurred are hard to reconstruct. Margaret's grim memories have been anaesthetised by the passage of the years. But it is clear that Bishop Rocksborough

Smith followed Richard and Margaret across the Atlantic, no doubt crossing in greater luxury than that provided by the simple cabins of the Manchester Port, on one of his regular fund-raising trips to the old country for his penurious Diocese of Algoma. He came to St. Laurence, clad in the grandeur of his episcopal gaiters. There he persuaded Richard to return to Canada, where, within months, he would have to leave Mindemoya and take up a new post as director of a campaign, to be called The Archbishop Thorneloe Memorial Fund. The purpose of this was to raise $150,000, to provide a permanent endowment of the Diocese of Algoma. There was to be no home for him: he would have to live in the Toc H Mark in Toronto. Margaret had to stay behind in England, totally dependent upon her father-in-law, who generously agreed to give her a home and £1 a week to live on. We need to remember that at the time she was only 23 years old with two young children, Bess and myself, and about to give birth to Pat in June. Richard was not even allowed to remain with Margaret until Pat was born: by May 15th he was back on the Atlantic again, crossing from Liverpool to Montreal in the SS *Athenia*.

For the next two years Margaret remained in North Wingfield, with her three children, but without Richard, trying to understand and cope with the strange customs of her Derbyshire in-laws. They were desperate times for her, still remembered 70 years later with a kind of horror. Even with the best will in the world there was a deep chasm of misunderstanding and experience between her and her in-laws. "I was dumped upon them", she cried to me. "How on earth could I manage? I had never cooked on a coal stove in my life before!" Every afternoon she took long and lonely walks, with the two little girls in the pram, myself by her side, 'around the lump' i.e. down Little Morton Lane to the bottom of the hill, then up to the church and back, past the Gate Inn, to St. Laurence. Meanwhile Richard was thousands of miles away in Canada, completing the work on the church at Mindemoya, saying goodbye to many old friends and perhaps starting to battle with a bishop who, he was to discover, had totally lost the confidence and respect of the members of his diocese.

It is a difficult task to trace accurately the events of the next 18 months. Margaret's memories are confined to the lonely months of separation and exile in Derbyshire, where she was isolated and preoccupied with the care of her children. Otherwise we are dependent upon four sources of information: a precious collection of photographs that have survived over the years, the three small, but for us important, volumes of a diary that William kept of his trip with Elizabeth to North America from August to November 1936, some newspaper cuttings that refer to the ill-fated 'Archbishop Thorneloe Memorial Fund', and copies of relevant articles in The Algoma Missionary News.[29]

On his return to Canada in May 1936, Richard travelled immediately to the Manitoulin Island. Photographs exist showing him outside the churches at Mindemoya and Providence Bay that same month. In June he preached at a large gathering assembled at the War Memorial that had been erected in the middle of the road to the west of the township. [By 2002 this had been moved to a safer position by the side of the road.]

But then, for some reason, he headed west to Saskatchewan. In June we find him back at Fort Pitt for what was to be his final visit to the prairies. While Margaret was giving birth to Patricia, thousands of miles away in England, we have pictures of him riding horseback, clad in chaps and using a full western saddle, surrounded by members of the extended Pepper clan, which included Kathleen and Archie Symes, with Nat Hunt, Margaret's half-brother. Perhaps he needed to get away on his own to make up his mind what to do. The people of Mindemoya wanted him to stay with them, his bishop wanted him to run the endowment campaign, his beloved wife and children were thousands of miles away, and he had little money; he was therefore in an impossible dilemma.

By August 1936 he was back on the Manitoulin Island. An article in the Manitoulin Expositor for the 6th August helps us fill in some gaps in the story, but it also raises other unanswered questions. It is worth citing at some length:

---

[29] These have been supplied by the Archivist at Laurentian University in Sudbury, Ontario, with whom the papers of the Diocese of Algoma are lodged.

THE RIVER GOES ON

Mindemoya Parish Church celebrates First Anniversary.

The Church people of the Parish of Mindemoya with Providence Bay and Big Lake were astir at an early hour last Sunday morning. It was the first Anniversary of the Dedication of the Parish Church of St. Francis of Assisi. Earlier on in the week there had been a well-attended meeting of all Church people in the Parish Hall. The purpose of the meeting was to re-organize the work of the Church and to 'take stock'. Early in the meeting Mrs Arthur Cox was unanimously elected as the Secretary of the Church Council, charged with the task of writing and keeping the minutes of meetings, which are to be held once a month in future. After this was done the Revd. R.M. Taylor was asked to vacate the Chair for a few minutes and the Wardens took charge of the meeting. A vote of confidence in the Rector was unanimously carried. He was told that if he would consent to stay at Mindemoya for a further period of two or three years he would have the practical support of all present. Replying, Mr Taylor thanked the meeting and promised, with the Bishop's approval, to stay in Mindemoya. He said the Bishop had been staying at his parents' home in England in June, and had expressed a wish to Mr.(W) Taylor that his son would stay in his present parish. He said it would be good idea if all present, "forgetting those things which lie behind", were to re-dedicate themselves to the Glory of God. The following Sunday was the anniversary of the church's dedication and that would be a happy time for a personal dedication for everyone. The Revd. D. Clarke of St. Alban's Cathedral, Toronto, and Mr. J.H. Newton, (an eminent Toronto artist, who painted the canvas of St. Francis in the Church) also addressed the meeting. Mr Newton remarked that Mindemoya possessed one of the loveliest Parish churches he has seen on this side of the water.

Many matters came up from the agenda for discussion. It was reported by the Chairman that $500 had been promised towards the erection of a Vicarage by the Diocesan authorities in Sault Ste. Marie. The meeting decided to plan details for the new house at an early date. It was decided to have a separate fund for all the designated monies which might be received for the further endowment of the Church and the completion of the furnishings. At the end of the meeting, tea, cake and sandwiches were provided by the ladies of the church.

....After the service the congregation went down below to the Parish Hall, where a cheerful fire of logs was blazing in the baronial stone fireplace. Tables had been tastefully laid by the women of the W.A. the night before, and fifty people sat down and enjoyed a hearty breakfast, served by the same "good and faithful" women of the Church. There was a spirit of truly Christian merrymaking in the air. Church-people from different parts of the parish had an opportunity to talk to each other and compare notes. After the meal, those who smoked enjoyed their pipes and cigarettes, whilst the W.A. partook of the somewhat belated meal.

.....Mr and Mrs W.A. Taylor, of St. Laurence, North Wingfield, Chesterfield, Derbyshire, England, the parents of the Revd. R.M. Taylor, expect to sail from England at the beginning of August for Canada for a two months' holiday with their son. Mr. Taylor is a keen member of the newly-formed Algoma Association in the Chesterfield Archdeaconry, and hopes to make a tour through the Diocese to see for himself the work of the Church, upon which he will make a report when he returns.

Mr. W.A. Taylor is the Managing Director of Messrs. W.A. Taylor and Sons of North Wingfield. Whilst they are in Canada, Mrs Richard Taylor, the wife of the Rector of Mindemoya, will live in the old home in Derbyshire. On June 17ᵗʰ last, she gave birth to a daughter, Patricia, ("Pat"). She is enjoying her stay in the Old Land very much.

We note from this that Richard, as rector, was unanimously given a vote of confidence and told that if he would consent to stay at Mindemoya for a further period of two or three years he would have a new vicarage and the practical support of all present. In addition the bishop had expressed a wish to Mr William Taylor that his son would stay in his present parish. Then comes the cryptic comment to the good folk of Mindemoya that, *'It would be a good idea if all present, "forgetting those things which lie behind", were to re-dedicate themselves to the Glory of God'*. One wonders what lay behind this remark. Maybe to encourage him to stay, *'the meeting decided to plan details for the new (Vicarage) at an early date'*. Finally, we are told that Mr W. Taylor as *'keen member of the newly-formed Algoma Association in the Chesterfield Archdeaconry . . . hopes to make a tour through the Diocese to see for himself the work of the Church'*. Then there is the poignant footnote, *'Mrs Taylor will live in the old home in Derbyshire. On June 17th she gave birth to a daughter, Patricia ("Pat".). She is enjoying her stay in the Old Land very much'.* There is so much in this article that does not ring true with what we know was really happening.

Yet only two months earlier, in the Algoma Missionary News, (Vol.33. No 2, for May – June 1936), the establishment of the Archbishop Thorneloe Memorial Fund was announced:

It has all along been felt that Algoma had a moral claim upon the Church in Eastern Canada for the equivalent of the lacking initial endowment, and within the last two or three years this claim has been recognised by the Provincial Synod of Ontario, which has now authorized an appeal to the Church in the Province for an addition to our endowment funds of $150,000 .... This having now been done the Committee appointed to take charge of the appeal has begun its work. His Grace the Archbishop of Ottawa is President of the Committee appointed by the Provincial Synod. The Lord Bishop of Algoma is Chairman ...and a number of prominent Churchmen, both clerical and lay, are included in its membership. The Revd.R. M. Taylor, formerly of Mindemoya on the Manitoulin Island, has been appointed Director of the campaign.

We note therefore that Richard is described as *'formerly of Mindemoya on the Manitoulin Island'.* We can only wonder what was going on. Was the bishop being duplicitous, (which seems likely), or did he imagine that Richard could continue at Mindemoya and, at the same time, run the endowment campaign? A close study of William's diary, written during his visit to Canada that fall, gives a poignant record of what happened.

William and Elizabeth crossed the Atlantic in the same ship, the *Athenia*, which Richard had used just two months beforehand. On the 15th August, they arrived in Quebec, to be met by Richard and two friends (Messrs Ferguson and Smith), who travelled with them up the St. Lawrence River until the ship docked at Montreal two days later. From there they set off by car to the Manitoulin Island, a journey that was to take them three days, with stops at Ottawa, then to repair a puncture and also to visit the famous Dionne quintuplets (exhibited as if they were in a zoo). Eventually, on the 20th August, they caught the 4 p.m. ferry to the Manitoulin Island, having paused again on the way at Espanola, where William sensibly fortified himself for the forthcoming adventure by buying a quart of whisky. Immediately, on arrival, they went to have a look at the church. William writes, *"Found it much better that expected. We were deeply impressed. Then we went to a Picture held in the school. It was a real talking picture."* Next day he was able to add, *"everything is better than I thought it would be on the island."*

The next ten days were fully occupied as William and Elizabeth were introduced to various parishioners, explored the island and tried to accustom themselves to strange Canadian mores. William's comments are fascinating:

"23 August. Went to 8.0 service this morning at Mindemoya and on to Providence Bay for 9.30, which was 10.0 when we got there. 11.0 service at Mindemoya. 7.30 evening service.

"25 August. We heard there was a pow-wow meeting, so we decided to go to a place occupied by Indians called Wikwemikong. ... We were initiated into the Indian rites . . . and shook hands with the Indian chief. They danced around us and made glee, chasing away evil spirits. They particularly liked our cigarettes."

The next day Mr Berry started work on a 'bishop's chair' that William had decided to present to the church. Then *"we took a run round Mindemoya Lake and saw where Dick and Margaret lived, in a small log cabin or house."* After this they *"went to the dance . . . bought hot dogs. These are made up of a baked bun and a sausage laid in, with seasoning."*

On the 29th August *"Canon Colloton called at our digs.* [He was to remain a staunch friend and ally of Richard throughout the years, eventually preaching at the consecration service for St. Francis Church in 1945]. *He told me what a fine job (Richard) had made of the Church. We motored to Little Current with him. We had a long talk and he thought Richard was a marvellous young man . . . I went to the bank to change a cheque. I realised $5.1 for the £."*

On the 31st August they left for Toronto. Richard travelled with them. He was to spend his time *"moving around the city begging for the Church."* He returned to Mindemoya on September 4th, leaving his parents to follow him later. On their return they found that Mr Berry had finished the bishop's chair. *"It is done and looks quite nice."*

During this critical period, Richard must have made up his mind that he had to leave Mindemoya. On the 10th September William records that *"Dick saw the auctioneer about selling his furniture etc."* At the same time he notes that *"The Bishop is due at Sault Ste. Marie today."* Thus Margaret was unable to take any part in the sale or transfer to England of any of the few precious household effects that she and Richard had managed to collect together in the early years of their marriage. For better or worse many precious Canadian artefacts ended up in a pseudo- log cabin that William constructed in a corner of the garden at St. Laurence on his return to England.

On September 11th he and Elizabeth *"stayed in and sorted out all the books Dick required to take home and packed them. He is advertising all his other goods in the Gore Bay Recorder next week. Ma has been sorting things out in Dick's room today."*

Thereafter events moved swiftly. Plans were made for William and Elizabeth to travel by train to Toronto and then on to New York, where they had arranged to stay with relatives, the Frelino family. Meanwhile Elizabeth spent her day (19th September) *"helping at the church, cleaning brasses, etc. She is saying she wishes the church was nearer. She would look after it."*

On the 21st September a happy day was spent fishing off Treasure Island in Lake Mindemoya, when no less than 66 fish were caught. It was a record for the season. One of them weighed 5 lbs – the largest caught that season. It was carefully stuffed and, in due course, shipped to England where, for many years, it was displayed as a proud trophy in William's log cabin. He was immensely proud of his achievement that day. *"I told them when I go fishing I attend to the job in hand."*

But, sadly, the visit to Mindemoya was to end on a sour note. Leaving the island on the 28th September the party, which included William and Elizabeth with Richard and some friends, set off for Bracebridge (a town in northern Ontario on the road between Toronto and North Bay), where the bishop lived. It was a journey of 323 miles. *"We arrived at 5.30 pm. The bishop had gone to a service at Uffington. Dick and his friends motored back from here and I stayed the night to see (the Bishop) in the morning".*

On the 29th September a painful interview took place between the two men.

"I went to the bishop. Could not get him to say yes. Later I saw Mrs Smith (the Bishop's wife). She does not like Dick leaving, but will do what she can. I have been hanging around Bracebridge all day. (The bishop) is a miserable man. This has not been a pleasant day for me and I know Ma will have been worried. I could have spared any day away from the Manitoulin but this."

We shall never know exactly what was said or decided that fateful day. It seems that William could not persuade the bishop to leave Richard where he had been most successful. The lovely church of St. Francis at Mindemoya, and the Christian community he had founded there, was one of the greatest achievements of his life. But now he was forced to leave Mindemoya and become inextricably linked with a bishop, whose extreme churchmanship and foppish behaviour undermined any chance of success for the endowment campaign to which Richard was now committed.

Nevertheless William and Elizabeth much enjoyed the rest of their holiday which was spent in New York. They stayed with Gabriel Frelino, who had married one of William's half-sisters. [His daughter Grace Frelino was later to be a somewhat exotic member of General Eisenhower's staff in Europe during the Second World War]. With him they saw some of the strange delights the 'Big Apple' had to offer: movie picture shows, the Ziegfeld Follies, skyscrapers, zeppelin flights overhead, news of the relationship between King Edward VIII and Mrs Simpson and, then at the beginning of November, they stayed up late one night to listen to the broadcast of the election victory of F.D. Roosevelt. Indeed there was so much to do that they delayed their return to England, arriving at Chesterfield on the 10th November, where they were met by John Mottershaw and Richard, who had crossed the Atlantic in the Queen Mary for a brief furlough, a month earlier.

Returning to Canada at the end of 1936, or early in 1937, Richard made his home at Toc H in Huron Street, Toronto. There he would have been supported by the companionship of the other young men who lived there. The offices of the endowment campaign were not far away at Church House on Jarvis Street. In addition, the artist Jim Newton, and his family, who knew Mindemoya, were good friends and lived in the city. Meanwhile the work on St. Francis continued. Photographs, dated August 1937, show it virtually complete in all its glory, with new choir stalls added. Earlier that year we can see Richard, the 'sky pilot' as he called himself, visiting the more remote parts of the diocese up on the line of the Algoma Central Railway at the Oba Lake Air Base, where Canadian Air Force planes, equipped with floats, were being used to survey uncharted territory.

That same summer the Algoma Endowment Campaign was officially launched. It was named in memory of the much-loved Archbishop George Thorneloe, who had died in August 1935 at the age of 87. A powerful letter from the Archbishop of Ottawa endorsed the campaign.

Archbishop Thorneloe Memorial Fund

August 10th 1937

Diocese of Algoma

For many years past, under each and all of the Bishops who have presided over the Diocese of Algoma, the financial condition of the Diocese has caused very great concern to all who realize the necessity of maintaining the ministrations of the Church throughout that great area.

In April 1933, under the auspices of the Provincial Synod of Ontario, an inquiry was made into the conditions under which the Diocese was founded, the assistance then promised towards its maintenance, and its present financial needs.

As a result of this inquiry the Provincial Synod in 1935 endorsed the principle that the Diocese of Algoma had a claim for financial assistance from the Ecclesiastical Province of Ontario, and from other Dioceses that took part in the founding of the Bishopric; and determined that an appeal should be made as soon as possible after the completion of the Restoration Fund.

In 1937 the Council of the Provincial Synod resolved that the appeal should be made in the years 1937 and 1938.

Committees have been duly appointed to carry out this resolution.

I desire now, as Metropolitan, to endorse the appeal that is to be made, and to commend it heartily to all who will take part in fulfilling a responsibility which I feel that we all share.

I pray that this effort long overdue may meet with full success.

John Charles Roper.   Archbishop of Ottawa

So a strong committee was formed, with Bishop Rocksborough Smith as chairman and with other members, such as the Dean of Toronto and Richard's close friend, Canon Fred Colloton, as colleague and advisor. Richard's role was to be the director.

Right from the beginning the bishop had clear and forceful ideas about how the campaign should be run, as the following letter to Richard indicates:

August 5th 1937

Dear Father Richard,

I am just off to Bracebridge for the Ordination, but I must send you a hurried line or two.

i.　　*I have just seen Dymond* (a leading Toronto layman). *He came to see me on Sunday after a Confirmation Service. He says he quite understands the situation and that he will do his very utmost to help us as he is quite keen on Algoma. Do use him as much as possible.*

ii..　　*I have sent Dr Boyle my criticisms on the letter headings. Will you discuss them with him? I think that the heading should certainly be –*
　　　"Archbishop Thorneloe Memorial Fund

Algoma Endowment Campaign.

iii..   *I think you should submit to me any literature you intend to issue.*

iv.   *Mrs Sullivan's letter should be helpful, but don't let it be too long. Ask her for a letter, and then make extracts from it – that is my advice. Old people are apt to be garrulous.*

v.   *Don't waste too much time careering about the United States. Our main field must be Canada. The Episcopal Church has a Forward Endowment Movement of its own. Don't waste <u>time</u> and <u>money</u> unless there is a very good prospect of a commensurate return. I think you should not go on <u>any</u> lengthy journeys without Dr. Boyle's approval.*

vi.   *A letter of introduction. I do not quite know what is wanted. Will the enclosed do? If so, please type it and send it to me for signature.*

vii.   *Keep Dr. Gould up to his offer of an office at Church House and try to get it <u>for yourself alone.</u> We don't want to be mixed up with any other cause, if it can be avoided.*

viii.   *Two things to be avoided -*
-    *Wild Goose Chases*
-    *Mare's Nests.*

Your affectionate Father in God

Rocksborough R:
Algoma

Almost immediately there were signs of trouble. A letter from Canon Colloton to Richard, dated the 21st August, commiserates with him by saying:

I am sorry you have met with such a discouraging reception in some quarters. It shows that the newspaper campaign waged by that confounded liar, W.J. Thompson, eight years ago is still remembered outside the Diocese, though his influence in Algoma is now almost nil. . . I am glad, however, that you had the courage to tell the Bishop, for he certainly ought to know what you are up against, and to realize that if the campaign should not be as successful as we hope it will be it won't be altogether your fault. He sometimes underestimates the antagonism he has aroused and it is well for him to face the facts. But how strange it is that this "Romanizing Bishop" just three or four weeks ago received three persons from the Church of Rome here in the Sault, and is doing the same thing throughout the Diocese on his Confirmation tours...

Sincerely yours,
Fred W. Colloton.

A few days later Richard wrote a brave letter to the bishop that must have sealed his fate as far as his long-term future in the Diocese of Algoma was concerned. Reading the faded carbon copy, that has survived among his papers over the subsequent 66 years, one can only admire his courage. Here it is:

September 3, 1937

My dear Father in God:

I do not like troubling you as I know you will be very busy at General Synod, but I feel that I ought to tell you what has transpired at a two hour interview with a Mr. Venables (a prominent and wealthy layman of the Diocese of Toronto) this morning.

Dr. Boyle was very keen that I should see Mr. Venables; he is of our school of churchmanship and a man of a good deal of influence in financial circles. I cannot help but feel it would have been better for someone much my senior to have told you these things but I know you will appreciate my frankness and the spirit in which it is written.

This is something of what Mr. Venables has in mind and I give it to you in a rather disjointed fashion. He is sure that the laymen of the province are very disturbed about Algoma. Before any campaign was launched the Diocese of Algoma should have put its own house in order, the laymen should have been organized.

During the time you have presided over the destinies of the Diocese nothing has been done to increase the capital funds. Money has been begged in England to keep the show running but there has been a great deal of frittering of effort and nothing concrete has been done. On the whole the clergy and laymen are loyal to you but you have not their respect.

It appears to Mr Venables that you have gone out of your way to antagonize the people of the province and to perpetuate undesirable party antagonisms in the Church. The whole situation in Algoma he finds very disquieting.

After I spoke to Mr Venables last night on the telephone arranging the interview he went over to discuss the matter with Provost Cosgrave, who apparently agreed with what Mr. Venables said to me. He, Mr.Venables, thinks you have failed signally to understand the outlook of Canadian people. He thinks that if one or other of two things were done the laymen of the province would arise to a man and the desired Endowment for the Diocese would soon be forthcoming. He, himself, could raise thousands of dollars. The two things are these: (1) that you tell the House of Bishops of the General Synod that you have come to the conclusion that your efforts to make Canada Catholic [i.e. Anglo-Catholic] have been along too hasty lines and that a spirit of tolerance will mark your future actions. (2) that you resign and make room for a man who will command the respect and love of the majority of his people.

He feels that you have been ill-advised by those closest to you.

I pass these observations on to your Lordship without comment, as such from me would be impertinent and out of place, but I find that this feeling is very general even among Catholic laymen and I am very disturbed.

114

Your affectionate Son in Christ,
R. M. Taylor. (Director)

Surprisingly the bishop seems to have ignored this letter and responded as if nothing untoward had happened. By November he was writing to Richard, full of plans for a visit to Toronto and a special Christmas appeal for the fund. But contemporary newspaper cuttings show how little he was in sympathy with those who controlled the purse-strings at that time and the real sources of wealth in Algoma – its mines and timber companies. *"The former lumber centres were "dead" with most of the houses closed up, as were former paper-making towns, but there were sufficient people left,"* he is reported as saying to The Toronto Globe and Mail on December 6th 1937. Then he added *"the mining centres are really more of a liability than an asset . . . the money made from mines came down to shareholders in Toronto, Montreal and other cities."* Deep down he couldn't understand the rough and ready ways of Canadian workers. The Toronto Daily Star, for the same day has him stating that *"Mining camp workers are often rather gay though I don't agree that they are lawless. Lumber camps are giving way to mining camps – and mining camps aren't very often religious."*

What would seem to have been the final straw that broke the camel's back was his behaviour during a series of elegant receptions and tea parties that were held in his honour in Toronto during a fateful visit to the city at the beginning of December. With an attention to the detail of fashions and flower arrangements that I find extraordinary the Globe and Mail reported that:

"Mrs H.D. Warren of "Red Gables" entertained delightfully at tea yesterday afternoon in honour of the Bishop of Algoma and Mrs Rocksborough Smith of Sault Ste. Marie. Mrs Rocksborough Smith, in pretty fuchsia chiffon and pearls, received with her hostess, who was gowned in black chiffon and lace. His Lordship the Bishop also received. The Diocesan Cross of brilliants . . . was worn by the Bishop and much admired by those interested in Episcopal jewellery. . . .Calla lilies in a large celadon centred the tea table, and chrysanthemums were used throughout the downstairs". And of course the good folk of Toronto were glad to know that *"Mrs R.Y. Eaton at Mrs Warren's tea looked*

very pretty in a smart gown and hat of burgundy red hues." Perhaps the ordinary folk of the diocese were none too amused at reports of such behaviour. In the isolated lumber camps, mining towns and agricultural communities, such as those on the Manitoulin Island, there was not much room or need for chiffon, cella lilies and episcopal jewellery.

The general chairman of the campaign, no less a person than the Archbishop of Ottawa, became alarmed when the suggestion was made to import, at great expense, a firm of fund-raisers from the U.S.A. In his own hand he wrote to Richard, on January 13th 1938, *"Would a high pressure campaign be more likely to succeed just now?"* Richard's good friend, Canon Colloton, added his own sarcastic comments eleven days later:

> *I am sorry to hear that the Bishop made such a mess of things at Mrs Warren's. If the Primate and the Committee agree that things are hopeless, I don't see what we can do but drop the whole Campaign. When a Bishop is guilty, or even accused, of heresy or immorality, there is a regular method of dealing with the matter under the Provincial Canons; but when he is guilty of the more serious crime of lack of tact there doesn't seem to be any way of bringing him to book, except punishing the innocent Diocese, and helping to starve the clergy.*

> *I believe you are trying to arrange a meeting of the whole Committee soon, to consider the American firm's proposition. The Bishop should take the leading responsibility in saying whether the campaign should go on or be called off, and whether we should risk $5000 plus in the proposed new venture. Personally I don't believe even W.W. & D. could make headway against the opposition we are up against.*

> *.. with heartfelt sympathy with you in your impossible task and many discouragements.*

> *Fred. W.*

Colloton

It seems clear that the bishop had totally lost the trust and confidence of his clergy and the people of his diocese. Two days later even he was forced to admit:

"I am coming to the conclusion that it might be not so impossible to postpone the appeal for a few years, in view of the fact that, as the Archbishop says. "we cannot succeed by overpressing the appeal at a time when other claims are calling urgently".

On the same day Canon Colloton wrote expressing his concurrence with this decision:

I learn from the Bishop that the Metropolitan thinks it might be well to postpone the whole campaign indefinitely, as there are so many conflicting appeals at the present time. There may be something in this. The passive resistance we are up against, the lukewarmness of Church people generally, and other matters, which I needn't mention, have combined to make the effort a failure. It might be the most dignified thing to drop it, but to leave it open to be renewed at some future time if circumstances became more propitious...

I wish I could see you and have a good talk, but I shall have to sit tight here for the present. Certainly the Bishop, and not I, should attend the meeting of the Committee, for an important decision will have to be made, and I am not hankering after that responsibility.

With kindest regards,

Fred. W. Colloton

So the die was cast. A telegram from the archbishop to Church House, dated February 18th 1938, said:

Agree campaign must be postponed. I wish to express to . . Mr Taylor my appreciation of work done and sympathy for lack of success so far.

A week later Richard wrote to Bishop Rocksborough Smith:

My dear Father in God:

Dr Boyle tells me that my work in connection with the Campaign will be over the first or second week in March. The final meeting of the Sub-Committee is to be held next Friday. The Archdeacon of Chesterfield has work for me when I can return to England, and I must begin to make plans for the future.

I shall be glad if you would be so kind as to send me my Letters Dimissory and such other papers as may be needed to effect my transfer.

I hope I shall be permitted to do what I can for the Diocese of Algoma on the other side, and I want you to feel that you can call upon me to assist in anything that may be done in England to help the Diocese of Algoma. I have appreciated your Lordship's kindness and understanding sympathy during the last few months.

I have the honour to be,
Your Lordship's obedient servant,

Richard M. Taylor

By way of consolation The Algoma Missionary News for January – March 1938, in its record of Clerical Changes, reported that:

The Revd. R. M. Taylor has returned to England, having been offered a sphere of work in the Diocese of Derby, not far from his home. We regret his departure, and wish him every success and happiness in the Motherland. The Church of St. Francis of Assisi, Mindemoya, remains to us as an evidence of his zeal and ability. It is admired by very large numbers of visitors to the Manitoulin Island: and, more important, it is an inspiration to the people who worship there and who worked so earnestly for its erection. Mr Taylor was in charge of the Provincial appeal for the Archbishop Thorneloe Memorial Fund, and on the postponement of the effort was set free to return to England, where the good wishes of many friends will follow him.

In addition to this there were others who recognised Richard's courage and integrity throughout this sad tale of episcopal incompetence. We have seen how Canon Colloton understood his difficult position and did his best to support him. Among the few possessions that Richard managed to retain from this critical period of his life is a fine portrait of him, painted by the distinguished Toronto artist, Adrian Dingle. Presented to him by his friends and admirers, it hung over the mantelpiece in his study for the rest of his life.

For nine years Richard had worked ceaselessly for the cause of the Church in Canada, at no small cost to himself and his own happiness. It may have been some consolation to learn that when Bishop Rocksborough Smith made his next visit to England at the end of 1938 he did not return to Canada. Even though the Second World War did not begin until September 1939 he thought it was too dangerous to cross the Atlantic. Instead he devoted himself thereafter to the work of the Church Union – a society founded in 1934, dedicated to the defence and furtherance of High Church principles in the Church of England. Its patron was that arch-appeaser, Lord Halifax.

During the spring and summer of 1938 Richard and Margaret, with myself, Bess and Pat, were to enjoy a measure of domestic peace and stability at North Wingfield in Derbyshire. On the 21st April Richard received from Lambeth Palace his 'Permission to officiate' as a priest in the Province of Canterbury. This was issued under the provisions of the Colonial Clergy Act for an initial period of two years only. In those days the ecclesiastical authorities were suspicious of clergymen ordained in the colonies. For the rest of his life Richard was to labour under a false sense of inferiority: the tragedy is that this, together with a continued history of clashes with episcopal authority, left him with a 'chip on his shoulder' that was to affect his own ministry. Meanwhile, he found temporary employment on the staff of the parish church at Chesterfield, under the wise guidance of Archdeacon Dilworth-Harrison, who became a friend for life. 'Things were done properly' at that church, with all the ordered and dignified elegance of Anglican worship at its best – full of the 'beauty of holiness'. Meanwhile we children played happily with our Derbyshire cousins. There is a picture of all of us, naked except for Gordon, playing in the brook which flowed at the bottom of the field beyond the garden of St. Laurence. I have vivid memories of a water-pistol fight with the local village lads over the gate at the front of the house, with Gordon as a staunch ally and leader. For a short time Bess and I went to the local school.

But our time in Derbyshire did not last long. Later that summer the offer came through to Richard from the Revd. A.C. Brashaw, the rector of the Tarrant Valley group of parishes, near Wimborne in Dorset, to serve as his curate. A large house at Tarrant Keynston came with the job, together with a stipend of three hundred pounds per annum, Richard's first sizable income. In due course the whole family piled into a car, followed by a lorry, driven by John Mottershaw, on which were piled the few family possessions, together with a bag of Derbyshire coal, and the first of many long cross-country journeys were made, on old and winding English roads, down through the Cotswolds, to the utterly different world of a remote Dorset village.

10 Tarrant Keynston and the War 1938 - 45.

The river Tarrant is a tiny stream that runs for some 10 miles SE in a small valley of the Dorset Downs, from its source at Stubhampton near Shaftesbury to the point where it enters the river Stour near Spetisbury, not far from Blandford. I don't know what happens to it now, but during the early 1940s it had a propensity to dry up in summer, revealing strange secrets during the war, such as unexploded ammunition, or the decaying corpses of delicate trout. In spring, one of the village lads had showed us how to poach these by 'tickling' their bellies. Along the valley the river gives its name to a string of villages, some of them no more than hamlets. As Rena Gardiner writes in her book on the valley:

> *It is quiet region, without drama in either landscape or architecture; yet although each of the villages have a quiet similarity of setting they are quite different in character and appearance. All use the local materials – flint, cob, green and heath stones, brick and thatch – in an infinite variety of shapes and patterns... The hotchpotch of materials, mellowed by lichens and time, warmed by the sunlight, can look enchanting. Apart from the ghost of Eastbury House, there is not a mansion in the valley and few large houses. Many farmhouses and cottages have mediaeval foundations but there is little visible from before the 18th century.* [30]

Maybe these words do not do full justice to the historical interests in the valley with which Richard, in typical fashion, soon made himself well acquainted. His rector, A.C. Brashaw, looked after the villages at the head of the valley – Tarrants Gunville, Hinton, Launceston and Monkton – and lived in some style in an elegant rectory at Tarrant Gunville, just below the fine country home built by Josiah Wedgwood. Not far away were the remains of Eastbury House – the scene of wild parties held during the 18th century by Bubb Dodington, a friend of William Pitt the Elder. Richard seems to have been left on his own to run his end of the valley – Tarrants Rawston, Rushton, Keynston and Crawford. The last of these churches is now redundant, isolated among meadows

---

[30] *Dorset: Tarrant to Blandford.* Rena Gardiner. p. 1.

by the side of the river. It is still well worth a visit, as Simon Jenkins writes:

> *This place of ghosts lies at the end of a lane leading to a Georgian farmhouse and outbuildings. It was the site of one of the richest Cistercian monasteries in England, founded in the 1220s by Bishop Poore, builder of Salisbury Cathedral, who returned to be buried. Here too lay Queen Joan of Scotland, daughter of King John of England.*[31]

My earliest memories of that little church are more prosaic. Not long after we had moved to Keynston, Richard took the large choir he had quickly established to sing at the funeral service in Crawford church for one of its leading farmers whose surname was Tory. How awed we young children were to be told that he had died while lifting his tractor!

Tarrant Keynston in 1938 was a long straggling village with a pub at one end, called 'The True-Lovers Knot', where the road from Blandford to Wimborne descends into the valley. A little further along the village was the infant/primary school that Bess and I, and later Pat and Mary, attended. Then there were two large houses – the Lodge where the Biddlecombe family lived (of which much more later) and a mansion, next door to the rectory, belonging to the Chapmans. Mrs Chapman objected strongly to the close proximity of the rectory washing line. I was more delighted when Mr Chapman's extensive model railway layout came my way one Christmas Day.

Even though Richard's title was 'Assistant Stipendiary Curate' our house was called The Rectory. It was a Georgian house with a rather ugly late-Victorian addition and impressive gables, one of which dominated its front and overlooked a drive. At the entrance to the drive was the little thatched gardener's cottage, inhabited by a cantankerous character called Charlie Bridle, who objected strongly to the presence of children in the walled garden. His son, Harold, was more sympathetic: he was a woodsman whose skill at making hurdles out of the hazel cuttings from local coppices was a source of endless fascination to me. On the southern end of the rectory there was a large collection of rooms below the

---

[31] *England's Thousand Best Churches.* Simon Jenkins. p. 162.

nursery wing – a kitchen, several sculleries and outhouses, in one of which was a large diesel engine, used to pump up water from the well. For many years Margaret had to wrestle with its idiosyncrasies and the peculiar problems of cooking on a paraffin stove because there was no electricity. At dusk, the candles or Tilley (paraffin) lamps were lit, their gentle hissing sound a background to evening activities devoid, of course, of television; instead the radio was our link with the outside world. To help her run this enormous house, of some 17 or 19 rooms, Margaret had the assistance of a live-in maid, who was expected to change at tea-time into a mob-cap and frilly apron. It was a far cry from the honest simplicities of life on the Canadian prairie or Manitoulin Island.

Soon after our arrival I was discovered playing in the middle of the drive at the front of the house by no less a person than Mrs Edith Biddlecombe from Tarrant Keynston Lodge. She had called to discover what the new family at the rectory was like. In my memory of that moment she closely resembled what I imagined Queen Victoria looked like – a short, dumpy figure, clad entirely in black – the widow's weeds she wore until her death, twenty years later, in 1958. But, for better or worse, she was to have a profound influence upon the family and especially upon Richard himself. Edith Biddlecombe's husband, Ernest, had just died. He had been a successful lawyer from Ormskirk, near Liverpool, who had retired not long before to Dorset, but his early death had left his widow stricken with grief. She was trying to cope with the task of looking after two daughters, Elizabeth (Betsy) and Anne, still not married, nor likely to be, and one son, John, recently returned in some disgrace from a failed career as a coffee planter in Kenya. A woman of deep faith, she turned to Richard for help. Naturally he responded as best as he could and soon a deep bond of affection arose between them. At that time he was a dynamic young priest, in his mid 30s, full of energy and enthusiasm and only too glad to turn Edith's grief into more positive channels. Such was the depth of their affection for each other that when Richard and Margaret's fourth child was born in October 1939, she was christened Edith Mary. The Bishop of Salisbury, Neville Lovett, chose to celebrate this event by calling at the Rectory in his chauffeur-driven Daimler and suggesting to Margaret, still in childbed, that perhaps in future she should limit her family. To Richard he observed that maybe he should economise by selling the Remington typewriter he had noticed on the study desk. It was another of the episcopal interventions that frustrated and angered Richard over the years.

Meanwhile the clouds of war were gathering fast. At the end of September 1938 the Prime Minister, Neville Chamberlain, had returned from a meeting in Munich with Hitler bearing proudly in his hand a piece of paper and proclaiming that this meant 'Peace in our time'. Disillusionment quickly followed. Not even the folks in Tarrant Keynston could ignore the preparation for war. On 31st January 1939 Richard received a letter from the commanding officer of No 142 Squadron R.A.F., based at Andover, thanking him *for the very valuable assistance which you rendered to Sergeant Jenkins and the crew of the aeroplane which force-landed at Tarrant Keynston on the 28th January*. At the same time precautions were taken to protect the nation's artistic treasures from possible damage by enemy air-attacks. Hence, throughout the war, the walls of the rectory were decorated with some fine paintings transferred there for safe-keeping from the Russell-Coates gallery in Bournemouth. Among them was Frith's enormous and splendid painting of Ramsgate Sands.

On the 22nd March 1939 Richard enrolled as an A.R.P. (Air-raid Precautions Warden). Long before the mass evacuations started in August 1939 some rough evacuee children from danger-zones in towns such as Southampton arrived for a brief stay in the village. Clad only in my combination underwear, I was laid out upon the rectory dining table as a living model for first-aid practice. Looking back today, life at that time seems to have had a strange dream-like quality. The summer was long and hot, tennis was played on the lawn, William and Elizabeth came down from Derbyshire to stay. An early photograph shows William playing cricket, clad in collar and tie, wearing a panama hat, and wielding a fine cross-bat as he is bowled middle stump, with Bess as wicket keeper. Perhaps it was at the same time that the Mottershaws, with our cousins Gordon, Anne and June, came to stay with us: Gordon and I had much fun with my fine train set, while William drove down to Bournemouth and returned with my first tricycle. With my boyhood friends from the village I learnt to explore the delights of the river Tarrant, catching fish in jam jars, building dams, or wandering through the woods with homemade bows and arrows.

The dream did not last long. At the beginning of September 1939 German tanks invaded Poland and on the 3rd September war was declared. On the 10th May 1940 Holland and Belgium were invaded and, on the same day, Winston Churchill became Prime Minister. Just over a month later, on 17th June (Pat's 4th birthday) Richard wrote to the High Commissioner for Canada investigating the possibility of repatriating the family. The questionnaire which he received from the Third Secretary at Canada House was never completed. Perhaps Richard was persuaded to keep his family with him by the memory of the sinking of the Athenia in the Atlantic the year before and its reminder of a similar disaster which befell the Lusitania in the First World War, when a ship full of refugees was sunk. In any case the prospect of sending Margaret, with four children, to live with her Pepper relations in Canada, was unimaginable. We remained in England to ride out the war as best we could.

In this situation Richard grew increasingly restless. All around him men and women were being called up to join in the struggle for the nation's survival. The Battle of Britain had begun on the 10th July and on the 14th August 1940 German aircraft attacked Southampton. What was he to do? Naturally he volunteered to serve in the armed forces as a chaplain. An initial overture to the Royal Navy met with a discouraging response, as Richard wryly recalled to me many years later, when I became a naval chaplain: "The Chaplain of the Fleet presents his compliments, but the Navy already has a full quota of chaplains." The Bishop of Salisbury clearly indicated that Richard's patriotic duty lay in ministering to the needs of his rural parishioners.

By October 1940 the Battle of Britain was over and with it the immediate threat of invasion was lifted. But the Blitz continued with an increasing number of night attacks, causing immense damage and inflicting numerous civilian casualties, particularly in London. On 26th September a surprise raid on the Spitfire factory at Southampton (only some 30 miles away from Keynston) stopped production of aircraft for some time. To add to the pressures put upon Richard, a trickle that soon turned into a flood, of gallant men and women began to arrive in the house. They were only too happy to find in a Dorset country rectory a refuge, a home-from-home and a ready welcome. Among them were Mildred's husband, Dennis Taylor, fellow Canadians such as Bill Blackstock and Ray Malarkey, and Richard's cousin, Grace Frelino, from New York. After Pearl Harbour, on 7th December 1941, and with it the entry of the U.S.A. into the war, these 'colonials' were joined by a host of Americans, who filled the rectory with their laughter and almost overwhelming generosity. Those were the days of food rationing, so I shall never forget my first taste of peanut butter, the intense sweetness of American candy, or, on one never-to-be-forgotten moment, the arrival at a picnic on Badbury Rings of some immaculately clad American officers with a whole tin of biscuits and other goodies.

In June 1941 sad news had arrived from Canada: Margaret's father Fred had died. Many years later Richard's successor at Fort Pitt, the Revd. Arthur Lea, came to live at Salisbury, and thus was able to talk to Margaret about it. In 'Fort Pitt History Unfolding' he writes:

> *It was June 1941 when I arrived at the parish then comprising Fort Pitt, Deer Creek, Frenchman Butte and Harlan. It was not long before I was plunged into Church life. I was told that a certain Fred Pepper was very ill and not likely to live long. The old farm was barely a mile from the Mission House and was the only inhabited building that I could see from it. As I followed the trail up to the house, I met a car, which proved to be the doctor's, coming from the house. He said he did not think Mr Pepper could last more than another 24 hours. I went in and within five minutes there was a stir in the sick room. Someone went in - probably Rose or Bill – and came out again with the words, "I think he has gone". This was the nearest I had ever been to the last moments of a dying man. But, calmly, I felt I could assure Mrs Pepper that it was so. Death had come so easily to this pioneer of the Canadian West.*[32]

At about the same time the question arose, 'What should be done about the children's education?' In March 1941 I was eight years old and in the normal course of events could expect to remain

---

[32] Fort Pitt History Unfolding page 184,5.

at the village school until I was 11, when I would either transfer to the secondary school at Spetisbury, where children left at 14, or possibly gain entry to the grammar school at Blandford. For one reason or another neither of these solutions was considered satisfactory. Then, with an astonishing act of generosity, that was to have a profound effect upon our destinies – both positive and negative – Edith Biddlecome decided to fund our education in the private sector. I was to be sent away, first to prep school, and then to public school; later, when the time was right, the girls would also go to boarding school. I shall never forget that moment when Edith peered at me over her half-lenses and declared with deep conviction, "God has told me not to spend my money on a memorial to Ernest, but on your education". It was a moral burden laid upon my boyhood shoulders that at times came close to destroying me. Margaret took no part in this decision: if Richard wanted something that was it: he naturally rejoiced that we should have the chance of a good education that had been denied him. But the emotional costs were enormous. For the next ten years, for the greater part of the time, I lived away from home. Terry Stone, my boyhood friend at Keynston, with whom I had made bows and arrows in Ashley Wood, or happily tried to dam the river down at Tarrant Crawford, now turned away from me in disgust. Henceforward we were strangers in the village, alienated by education from the country folk, and isolated from the 'bourgeoisie' by the knowledge that at home there was a constant lack of money that led to numerous domestic rows and arguments.

Throughout the summer of 1941 the search for a suitable prep school for me continued. I shall never know why, and to this day regret that, I was not sent to one of the many fine schools nearby in Dorset. Instead a ghastly place, called Park House School, was found for me at Paignton in Devon – a whole day's journey away, involving at least two changes, at Templecombe and Exeter, by rail, or a long sick-making coach journey. Perhaps it was felt that in faraway Devon I was unlikely to be bombed by enemy aircraft. Sometime in September 1941 a shopping trip to Bournemouth took place from which I returned with that essential item of schoolboy kit, a tuckbox. Then it was off to Paignton to be kitted out in all the glory of school uniform, when it was discovered I had one shoulder lower than the other; apparently I had been dropped as a child and broken my collar-bone. Soon all the pains of homesickness, from which I and subsequently my sisters also suffered, descended upon me. For the next five years, with all the drama of the Second World War a threnody in the background, I endured the nightmare of that English prep school. The headmaster was a loathsome bachelor, whose beatings during French lessons left me with an abiding hatred of learning languages that nearly ruined my subsequent academic career. To this day I can recall the delight at returning home for Christmas, to be greeted by my three sisters, among them little Mary, just over two years old, and running along the dark corridor that lay behind the dining-room and crying out, "Bull, Bull".

There were other moments of light in the darkness. For many years we celebrated Christmas with the Biddlecombes. Mary Coleman, at Church Farm next door to the rectory, would provide an enormous tea with wonderful trifles, and there were trips to the pantomime at the Pavilion in Bournemouth. For Richard the arrival, in October 1941, of his permanent licence to exercise the office of priest from Cosmo Gordon Lang, the Archbishop of Canterbury, must have given him a greater sense of security. For myself, my 9th birthday in March 1941 was a memorable occasion celebrated by the arrival at school of a chocolate cake from home, lovingly prepared by Margaret, using her meagre food ration – its icing made with dried egg powder a delicious crust to crack.

1942 was to be memorable for Richard for the arrival upon the scene of two men who were to have a permanent influence for good on his life. The first was William Temple, Archbishop of Canterbury from February 1942 until his sudden (and devastating for the Church of England) death in September 1944; the other was the gallant figure of Pilot Officer Paul Gibbs, who was a young Canadian from Harlan near Fort Pitt, whom Richard had prepared for Confirmation many years earlier. Of William Temple it could be said, without contradiction, by his biographer in 1948:

It is safe to say that, under any system of election or appointment, by Church or State or both, the choice would have fallen on Temple. No other bishop possessed in equal measure his many qualifications – a temperament exactly adapted to varied human relationships, unusual stamina, immense powers of concentration, a conveniently mediating mind which was yet without smudges, exceptional lucidity in teaching and speaking, a deep devotional life, a wide knowledge of the history of Church and State, a great reputation among the continental and American Churches and in the Anglican Communion overseas, and a fund of learning on which he seemed at all times able to draw with accuracy and ease. He was the most enlightened bishop in the National Church.[33]

On a few brief occasions and during one of the darkest years of the War (1943) the paths of Richard and the Archbishop of Canterbury were to cross. He was one of the few bishops to have recognised in Richard those gifts and talents that, sadly, he was never able to realise in full measure.

Paul Gibbs burst upon the scene like a meteor in full flight: of him it could be said that he was a supreme example of those gallant warriors who rallied to the call to battle. He fulfilled so many of my boyhood ideals. We need now to pause to hear his story, told in his own words, and passed on to me by his widow 61 years later.

PAUL GIBBS   D.F.C., A.F.C.

I was born on 28th August 1917, the second son of William Gibbs and Lulu Candace on the Indian Lake Indian Reservation. Attended by Doctor Matheson, daughter of the Revd. John Matheson, pioneer and at that time, Indian Agent ....

When war broke out in September 1939 I was on a 30-day trek with pack-horses and a large party of hunters in the Northern Rockies. We heard the news on our one cumbersome portable radio. I determined to join up – hopefully in its airforce – as my Uncle, Paul Lewis, had done in the First War. I had always dreamed of flying as he had – and on fighters too. Disregarding the terrible side of war generally, I had always read avidly the exploits of Canadian airmen, especially in that First Great War.

---

[33] *William Temple.* Iremonger. p. 475.

THE RIVER GOES ON

… The call finally came in April, 1940, when I was on a bear hunt North of Mount Robson, working for outfitter Roy Hargreaves at this time…..In a matter of a very few weeks after solo on our Fleet Finch biplanes, on to Ottawa for advanced flying to Wings standard – our wings were presented by the Great Billy Bishop – an honour indeed. [Billy Bishop was one of the most famous allied pilots of the First World War].

Now off to fight the foe! But no – sent off to try to instruct others – when I was so little ahead of new pupils that I had little to teach them. But no choice, so to Saskatoon to teach first on Harvards, then Ansons and Cessnas. Over Christmas 1940 and into the New Year. Then to Dauphin, Manitoba, from where I managed to get on a draft for overseas. To Halifax and a slow convoy to Iceland – and a fast convoy two weeks later to Scotland. Another short period at Torquay before going either to bombers, day fighters or night fighters.

Another toss up – because of some test or other which said "Exceptional Night Vision" – I was sent to a Hurricane conversion unit and on to 87 Night Fighter Squadron. We were busy mostly on night trips – individually over occupied France. One night I arrived back late after shooting up Cherbourg Harbour to hear that Pearl Harbour had been bombed. My first reaction was "Good – now we will have more friends on our side".

During this period, I also flew on detachment from a small 400 yard grass strip on the Scilly Isles. The task was to intercept German reconnaissance aircraft going out into the Atlantic. But this period was more of a holiday than anything else.

Then, this routine came to an end in 1942 and we stopped flying in England and the Squadron was loaded on a ship to go someplace – where? We were not told and there were many guesses – Far East, Murmansk, around Africa to Egypt. In any event, we steamed south and after some U-boat attacks, ended up in Gibraltar. There after a brief period where we learned to drink duty-free gin, we flew off to Algiers early one morning to join the North African landings. From there, we made our way slowly eastwards to meet up with the 8th Army coming from Egypt.

10 Tarrant Keynston and the War 1938 - 45.

*One incident off the Algerian coast that I remember clearly. I chased –
alone – a Ju.88 on and on –finally at great distance I got one hit by
20mm on one of his engines and fire started. I watched crew bale out
and get safely in their rubber boat, I then thought about going 'home'.
Arrived back, landed and ran out of fuel before I could taxi in.*

*We saw the end of the Italian and German forces at Cape Bon in
Tunisia and then settled down to wait for the Sicily landings – I made
it to Sicily and there my war ended for a time after malaria etc. .. I
said good-bye to my Squadron and back – by air this time to England.
Two or three weeks' holiday and then to a Spitfire unit.*

*Joining 66 Squadron, which was then part of a Norwegian Fighter
Wing on the South Coast. This began a very busy period: sweeps and
escort work over France and dive-bombing of German rocket sites. Our
losses, mostly from ground fire, were fairly heavy. Finally D-Day and
the Allied landings. Our only losses that day were from our own ships
– coming back to England after covering the beaches.*

*After the beaches, we went over the Seine, on and on to Brussels – later
to Holland. Losing some friends on the way. Nothing lasts forever and
war finished in Europe. Back to London with my lovely new wife .. The
Air Force was kind enough to give me a DFC and AFC.*

Paul Gibbs came to see me at prep school in Paignton when
he was on honeymoon in nearby Torquay with his 'lovely new
wife'. In 2003, Terry wrote to me: "I asked the headmaster to phone
your father (to ask if we could take you out), but he was a narrow-
minded man to whom rules were rules". So I was left with just the
memory of a glamorous young couple and a fine balsa-wood model
kit of a Hurricane to make. Many years later, in October 1984, I was
able to visit Paul as he lay dying at the Middlesex Hospital and
then, not long afterwards, to officiate at his funeral at the RAF
Church of St. Clement Dane's in London. When those who were to
bear Paul's coffin reasonably requested if it could be covered with
the RCAF ensign the local chaplain at the church stiffly replied,
"Oh no! We only permit the use of the union flag". The service
proceeded with the coffin draped, as ordered, with the union flag.
At the end the bearers stepped smartly forward and, stripping off
the union flag, revealed below in all its symbolic glory the RCAF

ensign. Thus a gallant airman was carried to his eternal rest. Of him these words, written by a fellow pilot with the RCAF, John Gillespie Magee – a 19 year old American killed in December 1941, whose brother, Hugh, was my closest friend at Westcott House – are surely true:

> *Oh, I have slipped the surly bonds of earth*
>
> *And danced the skies on laughter-silvered wings;*
>
> *Sunward I've climbed, and joined the tumbling mirth*
>
> *Of sun-split clouds – and done a hundred things*
>
> *You have not dreamed of – wheeled and soared and swung*
>
> *High in the sunlit silence. Hov'ring there,*
>
> *I've chased the shouting wind along, and flung*
>
> *My eager craft through footless halls of air.*
>
> *Up the long, delirious, burning blue*
>
> *I've topped the windswept heights with easy grace*
>
> *Where never lark, nor even eagle flew.*
>
> *And, while with silent, lifting mind I've trod*
>
> *The high untrespassed sanctity of space*
>
> *Put out my hand, and touched the face of God.*[34]

It is most likely that when Paul Gibbs turned up at Tarrant Keynston in 1942 Richard confided in him his deep frustration at not being able to serve with the armed forces, having been forbidden to do so by his bishop. "To hell with bishops!" was, I imagine, Paul's reply. Together they hatched up a plot. Richard donned a collar and tie (most unusually for him) and went to

---

[34] Reproduced by kind permission of The Revd. F. H. Magee.

10 Tarrant Keynston and the War 1938 - 45.

London to the RAF recruiting office. After due assessment he was granted a commission as a pilot officer in the Intelligence Branch. A uniform was ordered from the official tailor with a single stripe upon it and Richard was ordered to report for basic training. By this time the bishop had to be told. Another episcopal explosion ensued. "You can't, as a priest, serve as a civilian in the armed forces". Encouraged by Paul, Richard stood his ground until, with bad grace, the bishop accepted the situation and agreed to release him for service as a chaplain. Thus the uniform was returned to the tailor and an extra stripe was added to signify his immediate promotion to squadron leader – the relative rank carried initially by all RAF chaplains.

Richard's rector, A.C. Brashaw, was entirely supportive of the enterprise. Two significant letters from him, written in June 1942, have survived:

1. *Dear Taylor,*

    I enclose a letter which I think will safeguard your future position and put things right for your wife while you are away. Keep it safe somewhere as you never know what may arise! In lots of ways I envy you going.

    Yours, A.C.Brashaw.

2. *Dear Taylor,*

    In reply to your letter of June 8th and following our talk yesterday I write to say that I am quite prepared to release you so that you can take up a temporary chaplaincy with the RAF. After an extremely happy 4 years together I am very glad that you are prepared to come back when the war is over and in the meantime I shall be only too pleased for Mrs Taylor to continue living at the Rectory under exactly the same conditions with regard to Rates, dilapidations etc. Her kind offer of hospitality to any visiting Priest will help greatly with the new arrangement that I shall have to make.

    Yours, A.C. Brashaw.

THE RIVER GOES ON

For the next three years Margaret's 'kind offer of hospitality' extended to a whole host of men and women who stayed at the rectory. Among them were visiting clergy, engineers constructing the new airfield at Tarrant Rushton just up the valley and some servicemen who, to Richard and Margaret's utter consternation, discovered and read with glee a cache of early letters exchanged by them. [Margaret was later sad that Richard's impulsive reaction was to burn all these letters.] Eventually some order was established when an Australian woman, Eileen Jones, whose husband was serving with the RAF Intelligence Branch, came to stay for the duration of the war with her two young children, Gilbert and Susan. A friendly, efficient nurse, she and Margaret became good friends. On the feast of St. Michael and All Angels, i.e. 29th September 1942, Richard was at the RAF initial training school, Uxbridge, bearing with him so typically a copy of 'The Knapsack', Herbert Read's fine anthology of prose and verse. [It was intended to mirror a similar anthology, 'The Spirit of Man', prepared by the Poet Laureate, Robert Bridges, in 1916 for the same purpose.] I still have it in my library. On a more personal level, and equally typically, declared Margaret wistfully to me many years later, "He left me pregnant". A fourth daughter, Gillian, was to be born next year, on 1st June 1943.

The years in the RAF were good for Richard. He had rank and status, and the easy, egalitarian ways of war-time service life suited his rebellious nature. For a while he sported 'CANADA' tabs on the shoulders of his uniform, these made him a somewhat exotic figure. Soon he became a popular member of the team at RAF Detling, to which he was posted after his brief initial training at Uxbridge. It was a base for some fighter squadrons outside Maidstone in Kent engaged in the defence of the SE corner of England. In due course the county newspaper, the 'Kent Messenger', carried a fine series of cartoons depicting characters from the air station – among them is a good profile of Richard, alongside which is an apt description of his job (borrowed from the Navy) – 'Guide, Counsellor and Friend to all ranks'. True to his nature Richard immediately set about establishing a fine chapel in one of the airfield buildings. He persuaded no less a person than William Temple, the Archbishop of Canterbury, who had moved his diocesan residence from Canterbury a few miles inland to Maidstone for safety's sake, to come and dedicate it. On my study wall I have a precious photograph of that occasion - the gaitered, tubby figure of the archbishop smiling broadly at Richard, who stands among a group of fellow officers, while alongside the NCO commanding the guard of honour, tin-hat firmly on his head, stands poised and ready to take charge. For a few brief, precious months Richard felt that he was accepted by the man who was the ultimate source of authority in the Church of England. He and the Archbishop became friends, meeting (so Richard told me later) sometimes for coffee in Maidstone, when William's bellowing laughter, for which he was famous, could be heard echoing along the street.

At the end of May 1943 the Allied campaign in North Africa ended. A fierce battle to liberate the island of Sicily then followed (in which Paul Gibbs took part), before Montgomery's Eighth Army could cross the Straits of Messina as a preliminary to the occupation of the toe of Italy. At the same time the Italian forces signed an armistice. The tide of war was turning. Back home in England, 1943 was a momentous year for Richard and Margaret. Gillian was born on the 1st June. Not long afterwards Margaret broke her leg while cycling up the village – fortunately this took place outside The Lodge and Betsy Biddlecombe was able to rush out and administer effective first aid. Then, just as the long-awaited school summer holidays were beginning, Richard crashed in a small light aircraft on his way back to Detling, having hitched a lift down to Dorset to see his new daughter. He was lucky to survive because the aircraft crashed into a wood and he was rushed to hospital at Orpington in Kent with a fractured neck and severe wounds to his upper lip. In due course he recovered, but for the rest of his life he suffered neck pain for which he received a small disability pension. It was a frantic time for Margaret, unable to travel to Kent with a new baby and a broken leg; fortunately William was able to travel from Derbyshire to Kent to assess the situation.

Sometime early in 1944 Richard was summoned to the C.O's office at RAF Detling, where a puzzled Wing Commander Hawkins said to him, (as we were told later in a tale which lost nothing over the years), "Padre. I've got a draft order for you here. You've been ordered to report for duty at a brand new aerodrome that has just been completed at some God-forsaken place in Dorset called Tarrant Rushton. Have you any idea where it is?" With tongue firmly in cheek and unable to believe his luck, Richard replied, "I've no idea, Sir. I'll have to find out". Someone must have been pulling strings on his behalf. Was it Paul Gibbs up to his tricks again? Because we all knew where Tarrant Rushton aerodrome was – less than four miles away from Keynston and close enough for Richard to be able to live at home. Some of the engineers who had build the place were billeted for a time at the rectory: during the holidays I used to watch, with considerable fascination, the place being constructed with great diggers scooping up vast quantities of earth. With a happy heart Richard must have packed his bags, knowing that he had done a good job at Detling.

Richard received not long afterwards a letter from Ian White-Thompson, the archbishop's chaplain:

Lambeth Palace, S.E.1.   *Feb. 28th 1944*

Dear Dick,

Thank you for your two letters. I am so glad that you are settling down happily and that you are finding people friendly. If anything takes you in the direction of Yatesbury there is a very good Padre there called Collins[35]   - I have spoken to him about you in case there should be opportunities of contact . . . I have spoken to the Archbishop about your request, and he will gladly send a line of recommendation to the St.Brandon's School at Wells. . . We had quite a rough time in London last week, but the [anti-aircraft] barrage was a cheering spectacle.

All the best,

Yours ever, Ian White-Thompson.

As a result of this Bess and Pat were dispatched to St. Brandon's 'Clergy Daughters' School' in September 1944. During

---

[35] The later to be famous Canon John Collins of St. Paul's Cathedral. He stayed at Shroton in the summer of 1967.

The cousins on the veranda of Canada House, North Wingfield,
Derbyshire 1937
Gordon, Bill, Anne, Pat, June, Bess

Bill, Pat and Bess
4th January 1938

Tarrant Keynston Rectory 1940
Bess, Nanny, Margaret and Pat

Daddy Doe bowled middle stump!
Margaret, Pat, Nanny, Daddy Doe
Bess (wicket keeper)

Off to school 1944
Bill, Margaret with Gillian, Pat, Mary and Bess

Richard with Archbishop of Canterbury
Dr. William Temple
R.A.F. Detling 1943

GUIDE, COUNSELLOR,
AND
FRIEND, TO ALL
RANKS.

S/LDR R.M. TAYLOR

Richard 30th December 1942

UNITED PROVINCES

MUTTRA

Paul Gibbs R.C.A.F

Shroton Rectory 1946

Shroton Rectory 1960

The family in 1946
Mary, Richard, Margaret with Gillian, Pat
Bill, Bess

John 4th August 1950

John and Pat
11 April 1952

Pat and Mary
1947/48

Air Photograph of Hambledon Hill 1978
© University of Cambridge

the war it was housed in the Bishop's Palace at Wells before being transferred to Clevedon in Somerset in September 1945. Pat, in particular, never settled down to life at boarding school. Bess recalls how, during those first days at school, she had to suppress her own sorrow and help her homesick sister plait her hair in the mornings. She recalls how the whole ethos of the establishment was designed to subjugate any sense of self-esteem: the ideal set before the girls was that of the missionary or someone who married their father's curate, or both! To make matters worse the journey either to Wells or later to Clevedon was a hideous cross-country journey by rail, with changes, to get to the latter, at Evercreech, Highbridge and Yatton on the Somerset and Dorset Railway. Only on one occasion was Richard involved in these journeys when, with Paul Gibbs, he took the girls back to school: he was either away with the RAF or, later on, unwilling to involve himself in the miserable process. Indeed, throughout our years at boarding school we were largely left to fend for ourselves, as far as he was concerned – his own lack of formal education an obstacle in his dealings with teachers, housemasters, headmistresses and the like. It was Margaret who did her best to keep in touch with letters and parcels.

Tarrant Rushton airfield was constructed on the high ground to the east of the Tarrant valley, not far from the southern end of Cranborne Chase. In its early days the airfield was used as a base for light aircraft that could fly or parachute S.O.E. operatives into enemy-occupied Europe. [During the Falklands campaign of 1982, when I was chaplain at the Portland naval base, I was able to participate in the unveiling of a memorial commemorating their bravery. It is situated near what is left of one of the great hangars]. Directly facing the airfield across the valley was Blandford Camp, a large military establishment built in the First World War, when it was used by units such as the Royal Naval Division, one of whose most well-known members was the poet Rupert Brooke. Indeed his immortal poem – 'If I should die, think only this of me' was written from Blandford Camp while he was waiting to go out to Gallipoli. Dorset and most of southern England was a hive of military activity. Throughout the latter part of 1943 and the first six months of 1944 hundreds of thousands of men and women, from all units of the Allied forces, and the necessary equipment that went with them, were preparing for the long-awaited invasion of mainland Europe. Rural roads were ravaged by enormous vehicles: bridges were strengthened to bear the weight of tanks (one of which killed the rectory dog – Pax): the trains were so full of uniformed personnel that, on one occasion, when returning from school, I had to be bundled out of a train window by cheerful servicemen, there being no room to move along the corridor. The skies were full of aircraft, that I took a particular delight in identifying, some of which were towing gliders – Hengists and Horsas – until, by the beginning of June, all personnel were ordered to remain on duty at their posts. At Tarrant Rushton the tedium of waiting was enlivened by the arrival of war correspondents, among whom was an inebriated Ernest Hemingway.

On the morning of June 6th 1944, as we were lined up for our usual morning assembly at Park House School, one of our few day-boys arrived with the exciting news, "They've landed!" Thus I heard of the largest invasion in human history. It was D-Day: with it began the eventual liberation of Europe. It was an event forever etched into my psyche. That following summer holiday I was allowed to stick a map of Western Europe upon the kitchen wall at home and took great pride in up-dating it each day with coloured arrows and other symbols to mark the movement and disposition of forces involved in the epic battles. During that summer, after supporting the D-Day landings, the battleship *King George V* came to anchor in Torbay and we schoolboys were allowed on board for a visit. From this came a love for, and a pride in, the Senior Service (as it is traditionally called), that has never left me.

On 25th August 1944 Paris was liberated: nine days later British forces captured Brussels: soon it would seem that allied forces might be crossing the Rhine into Germany. Then came the disaster of operation Market Garden, when airborne forces, taking off from such places as Tarrant Rushton, found themselves landing, at Arnhem, in the middle of SS Panzer Divisions. With this set-back the pace of advance slowed down. At home concern was mounting about the state of the Archbishop of Canterbury's health. Retiring to the north Kent coast to rest his badly gout-infected legs, William Temple died suddenly, with little warning, at the end of September, of a pulmonary embolism. It was a devastating blow for the Church of England. Of Temple it could be said:

> *Many primates have ruled the Church with vigour and distinction, one or two have helped to determine the course of its history, and a few have wielded an appreciable influence over one section or other of the life of England. But of none, except Temple, since the Reformation, can it be said that the **world** was the poorer for his passing. The weight of his moral authority was equalled only by that of Franklin Roosevelt: its extent was unique... . To the common man his death was the loss of a champion and a friend.[36]*

It was also a devastating blow for Richard: gone now was the one man who might have been able to guide his paths when the war was over. What therefore was he to do? A natural part of his chaplaincy duties was a care and concern for the families and other dependants of service personnel engaged in the struggle. Thus he was lucky enough to be one of the few people to travel freely around Dorset, equipped with an ancient Lanchester car and an allowance of petrol. During these trips he was able to use his adequate chaplain's salary, and his jackdaw-like skill at detecting bargains, to build up the fine collection of clocks, furniture and pictures that was later to decorate the rooms of his country rectory. Frequently, to Margaret's chagrin, he would return home with some ancient artefact that had to be cleaned immediately on the kitchen table. Thus he carefully fostered the growth of the image of the Victorian clergyman and man-of-letters which later became so important to his sense of self-esteem.

More importantly, in the latter part of 1944, he found himself spending much time engaged with work for such organisations as SSAFA (Soldiers, Sailors and Airman's Families Association) and the Dorset Territorial Army Welfare Association. The president of the latter was a distinguished country gentleman called Sir Randolf Baker, Bart. He was distinguished by having lost an eye and gained a DSO during the battle of the Somme from which, so we children were told, he had been dragged off the battlefield by one of his retainers serving with him in the Dorset

---

[36] Iremonger pp. 627, 628.

Regiment. He and Richard seem to have developed a sense of mutual esteem and ability to work together. Randolf Baker owned a large estate at Ranston, in north Dorset, not far from Tarrant Rushston and, typically for the Church of England, was also patron of the local living at Shroton, or Iwerne Courtney, nearby. At that time it was vacant and the rectory had been occupied by U.S. troops billeted there for pre-invasion training. Having enjoyed a measure of autonomy and freedom as an RAF chaplain, and now with a large family of five children to care for, Richard was no doubt reluctant to return to life as an assistant curate at Tarrant Keynston. It is not therefore surprising that he and Sir Randolf should discuss the possibility of a move to Shroton. Evidence for this comes in a letter:

November 25th, 1944

Ranston, Blandford.

Dear Taylor,

. . I had a talk this morning with our churchwarden and Mr Cameron, who is priest in charge here for the duration. They would like to meet you and talk over the prospect of getting you to come as our Rector after the European War is over. They all seemed much in favour of your coming. I expect you would like to see the Rectory and Church etc, and talk to them all. Could you come over one afternoon this week . . . about 3.30 and go round with them and stay to tea? I think it would be best, if I could write to the Bishop or see him, with the approval of the Churchwardens in my pocket.

If you would care to bring anyone with you of your RAF people, we should be delighted if they didn't mind walking around the place or looking at the house, while we were up the village . . .

Yours sincerely, Randolf L. Baker.

Thereafter events moved swiftly. On 4th December 1944 the Bishop of Sherborne wrote to Richard, while agreeing to take a Confirmation at Tarrant Rushton;

-   *'I am interested in what you write about Shroton but it will want some thinking about. I*

10 Tarrant Keynston and the War 1938 - 45.

can't help feeling that you ought to have a bigger population!'

Next day Sir Randolf Baker revealed that he had received an answer from the Bishop of Salisbury:

- *'He says that he will ask you to come and see him. He says undoubtedly an appointment rests with him now' [After the interregnum during the war years the right of appointment had by law lapsed to the Bishop].*

An interview with the bishop took place on Saturday 16th December, as a result of which ten days later Richard received a formal offer of the benefice of Shroton cum Farrington (a tiny hamlet about three miles west of Shroton).

....

The next year, 1945, was an extraordinary one for Richard and Margaret as the Second World War drew to its close.

In Britain and America crowds thronged the streets on 8 May to celebrate 'VE Day': in the Europe to which their soldiers had brought victory, the vanquished and their victims scratched for food and shelter in the ruins the war had wrought.[37]

On August 6th the first atomic bomb was exploded over Hiroshima and with the detonation of another, three days later over Nagasaki, the Second World War soon came to an end. VJ Day, August 15th, found the whole family, crammed into the ancient Lanchester car, driving through the devastated centre of the city of Coventry, on our way to a brief holiday in Derbyshire. Richard was still serving as a chaplain in the RAF, based at Tarrant Rushton and living in the rectory at Tarrant Keynston. An attempt had been made to institute him to the benefice of Iwerne Courtney (Shroton) on February 12th only for this to be cancelled at the last moment. This was the first of a whole series of tragic misunderstandings that was to have a disastrous effect on Richard's subsequent ministry in

---

[37] *The Second World War.* John Keegan. p. 533.

the Diocese of Salisbury. The Chaplain-in-Chief of the RAF, Archdeacon John Jagoe, who had become something of a personal friend, indeed he once visited us in Dorset, wrote to Richard in June, in response to a request for an early release:

> *If you can be inducted to your new Parish of Shroton while still in the Service – a thing which has frequently been done for other Chaplains – that will give you peace of mind and assurance as regards your future. This, as I say, has been done in many cases and has the approval of the Archbishops, but of course it remains in each case a matter for the particular Diocesan Bishop concerned, and naturally I cannot interfere.*

In August 1945 Richard was at last inducted into Shroton Church. But the family was still living at Tarrant Keynston. The rectory at Shroton was virtually uninhabitable, having been almost completely wrecked and vandalised by the soldiers who had occupied it during the war. Its doors had been used as dartboards and the garden littered with the remains of no less than five Nissen huts. In September Bess, Pat and I returned to boarding school from Tarrant Keynston for the last time. At the same time Richard received a letter from his former rector, A.C. Brashaw:

> *I am writing to let you know that I have heard today that Keynston 'Rectory' passes out of my hands on September 29th, which means that after that date I shall have no further say in the matter. If, by any chance, Shroton Rectory, is not ready for you by then, no doubt you will be able to make arrangements with Miss Joyce Wilson.*
>
> *Yours   A.C. Brashaw.*

His situation was desperate. To add to his problems he discovered that there was a lien on the benefice income of Shroton, in which he was liable to pay £150 per annum (out of a total income of some £350) for the pension of his predecessor, the Revd R.H. Gundry, who had retired years earlier. [The haphazard nature of the Church's finances at that time meant that there was a vast discrepancy in clerical stipends, which still depended largely on endowments and income from glebe lands etc.] A request from Mr Gundry's solicitors for a half-yearly cheque of £75 was passed on cheekily by Richard to the bishop for payment. The rebuke he received on December 4th must have shattered what little faith he had left in episcopal understanding:

> *The Palace, Salisbury,*
> *Wilts.*
>
> *Dear Taylor,*
>
> *I am somewhat annoyed at the receipt of a letter of which I send you a copy. I find that in my absence last September conversations and correspondence took place with you on the subject of the pension payable to Mr. Gundry. . . It is very unusual, in fact I have not known a case of it before, for any Incumbent–Designate to refuse to take information as correct from the Suffragan Bishop.. . It must have been obvious to you that I had made a mistake and I regard it as a great piece of impertinence on your part to tell Messrs. Andrews, Son and Huxtable [Mr Gundry's solicitors] to apply to me for future payments of the pension.. .*
>
> *You will remember that I spoke to you very seriously about being careful over your finances, and the way that you are acting in this matter does not make me very happy.*
>
> *Yours sincerely, Sarum.*

A posting that winter to serve with RAF forces in occupied Germany in the Hamburg area may have come as something of a relief. The move to Shroton had taken place in November. But Margaret was left to cope with life in a wrecked rectory, with a husband away in Germany, three children away at boarding school, and Mary and Gillian still at home. It must have been a desperate time.

11 Shroton 1945 - 1952.

The move to Shroton took place during my last year at prep school. With the ending of the war life at school became somewhat easier. Anti-tank barriers were removed from the beach at Paignton and we were allowed to swim in the sea. My headmaster began to behave like a human being by rescuing his beloved Bentley from the garage, where it had been preserved on bricks for the duration of the war. In this he took us for excursions on Dartmoor. But food was to be rationed for several more years and it was almost impossible to obtain building supplies for the necessary reconstruction of the rectory: nor, of course, was there much money available to pay for it. I was considered to be old enough to make my own way home by train from Paignton to Blandford. The final stage of the journey from Templecombe where I changed on to the Somerset and Dorset line (otherwise known as the 'Slow and Dirty'), was full of excitement. Puffing away busily, the ancient steam locomotive made its way through the Dorset countryside, halting sometimes apparently in the middle of fields at tiny centres of population such as Henstridge, Stalbridge, Sturminster Newton, Shillingstone and Stourpaine Halt. Peering out to the east, where sometimes my view was obscured by clouds of steam from the engine, I longed to see the familiar outline of Hambledon Hill. It dominated the landscape just as it dominated the lives and imaginations of Richard and the rest of the family in the years to come.

Hambledon Hill and the countryside surrounding it was the focus for an extraordinarily rich variety of historical events and personalities, as Richard was to discover and commemorate in his preaching, writing and story-telling during the next few years. They fed his imagination and focused his reading such that he was always reluctant to leave the place; indeed he was to remain there until his death 28 years later in 1973. Shroton and the lovely rectory, as it was gradually restored over the next few years, lay at the very heart of the family life that Richard and Margaret created together and brooding benignly over the house and village was Hambledon Hill with all its historical associations.

THE RIVER GOES ON

The church and rectory are situated to the east of Hambledon Hill, which is approached up one of its long flanks that overlook the Fairfield and the cricket pitch. As one climbs up to the rampart of the Iron Age fort at its north-western corner magnificent views over Blackmore Vale open up. These are framed on one side by the hills on the edge of Cranborne Chase leading up to Shaftesbury, while over to the west stretch the Dorset Downs with Bulbarrow as the highest point. At the foot of the hill on the western side the river Stour cuts its way through the Downs – a route to the sea at Christchurch guarded by the Roman fort on Hod Hill, just to the south of Hambledon. "Let's go up on Hambledon!" became the familiar cry of my youth. Up there I flew my first kite – an ex Air-Sea Rescue one liberated from an aircraft life-raft. Much later I was allowed to go shooting with my .22 rifle. Sometimes at dawn one would disturb the deer and one evening at dusk I felled at long range a fine hare. When my sister Pat worked as an assistant matron at Hanford School, over at the foot of the SW corner of the hill, I once walked her back to work in the snow. Afterwards I made my way home in the dark, pausing to listen to badgers crunching snails by an ancient clump of yews, one of the oldest in the country. This is the countryside described so well by Thomas Hardy: his novel 'The Woodlanders' is set not far from Bulbarrow and Tess of the D'Urbervilles must have walked past Shroton on her last sad walk from Marnhull to Old Sarum.

Archaeological excavations carried out by Roger Mercer of the University of Edinburgh during the 1970s have revealed that human occupation of Hambledon Hill began before the familiar ramparts of the Iron Age fort were constructed. During the Neolithic era (about 3000 B.C.), when Blackmore Vale itself was largely uncultivated woodland and marshes, our early ancestors lived up on the hill for safety from enemies and wild beasts. They disposed of their dead by exposing corpses to be eaten by vultures and carrion crows.

The main causewayed enclosure may have been the site of a gigantic necropolis constructed for the exposure of cadaveric remains

*of a large population . . . (at times) it was a vast, reeking cemetery, its
silence broken only by the din of crows and ravens.*[38]

At times Richard would wax lyrical about the possible
association of Hambledon Hill, and Hod Hill in particular, with the
Roman Empire and the early years of Christianity in the British
Isles. He may well have been correct. The Emperor Claudius
invaded Britain in 43 A.D. While he was still in the country

> *The future Emperor Vespasian (with the Second Legion) was
> campaigning separately towards the west fighting warlike tribes,
> among whom were the Durotriges of Dorset . . . we may perhaps
> visualize him fighting his way westward from hill-fort to hill-fort,
> supported along the coast by the fleet.*[39]

Did Vespasian ever meet or know about St. Paul? This was
the question Richard asked. [It is unlikely. Vespasian only became
Emperor in 69 A.D., in the Year of the Four Emperors, on the death
of Nero the year before. It was during Nero's reign that Christians
were persecuted, among them possibly St. Paul, after the Great Fire
of 64 A.D]. But certainly there is evidence that Christianity was
established early in this corner of the country.

> *By c. 330 – 340 not long after the conversion of the Emperor,
> Constantine, to Christianity, a portrait of a young beardless Christ had
> been set in a fine floor mosaic at Hinton St. Mary in Dorset (not far
> from Sturminster Newton): probably it derived from a church's
> decoration, a portrait, perhaps, in its dome. As yet, it is the one mosaic
> portrait of Christ which is known in a private house of this date.*[40]

[Appropriately enough this mosaic, which has now been
removed to the British Museum was found in the grounds of the
lovely manor house at Hinton St. Mary, whose occupant at that
time (just after the war) was George Pitt-Rivers. His father,
General Pitt-Rivers, was one the 'fathers of British archaeology'.
George was a maverick figure, one of whose hobbies, as

---

[38] *Hambledon Hill. A Neo-lithic landscape.* Roger Mercer. p. 63.
[39] *Oxford History of Roman Britain.* Peter Salway. p. 69.
[40] *Pagans and Christians.* Robin Lane Fox. p. 676.

described in Who's Who was 'baiting bishops'. Significantly he and Richard became good friends].

Meanwhile the stories continued, no doubt embellished over the years. But the telling of them and my own subsequent reading about them have ensured that this 'locus' has etched itself deep into the family's psyche.

Another significant episode took place on Hambledon Hill during the Civil War, when the Dorset 'Clubmen', who were fed up with the depradations wrought by the opposing forces of Charles I and Cromwell, declared a 'plague on both your armies' and rose up against them, armed only with primitive agricultural weapons. "One of their leaders was the rector of Compton Abbas" [just a few miles up the road towards Shaftesbury] declared Richard with a glint in his eye, "for his pains he was taken to Sherborne and hanged". I used to doubt his words until many years later I read:

> *In the counties of Worcester, Hereford and Dorset the last months of 1645 had brought a new element into the war. Plagued by the exactions of the armies, the assessments, the foraging and the billeting of troops, the country people – mostly yeomen and their sons, with some of the smaller gentry – were bonding together against both parties. These "clubmen", as they were commonly called, for the rank and file had no better arms, provided a warning signal for Royalists and Parliamentarians. . . They confronted the armies with the outcome of their failure: a widespread and growing movement to counter force by force, and to refuse further subsistence to the troops.*

> *(In August 1645) the "malignant clubmen" ... were active once again .... Colonel Fleetwood, sent by Cromwell with a troop of horse, surprised some of the leaders at Shaftesbury in consultation with messengers from the Royalists and carried them off as prisoners to the camp at Sherborne.*[41]

But it was the 18th century that perhaps most excited Richard's historical imagination. Just beyond Sir Randolf Baker's fine estate at Ranston lay another elegant demesne at Stepleton. [It is owned by the Earl of Crawford, who during Richard's time as

---

[41] *The King's War 1641 – 47.* C.V. Wedgwood. p. 403,404.

rector, leased the property to the distinguished Oxford numismatist, E. Stanley Robinson, who was one of Richard's close friends and supporters.] Stepleton House was built by the father of Peter Beckford, one of the most famous of English fox-hunters: his cousin was the notorious William Beckford, the builder of the extraordinary folly at Fonthill near Tisbury.

> *Peter Beckford married a Pitt heiress and their son took the surname of Pitt Rivers and succeeded to the Rivers estate and title. Peter was the author of 'Thoughts on Hunting'. Originally the main road [between Blandford and Shaftesbury] ran straight and close to Stepleton House: Beckford entertained the County Commissioner so magnificently that he readily signed a paper before he staggered to bed. When he woke up twenty-four hours later the straight road was blocked and the S-bends in use.[42] [as they still are to this day].*

Between them the Beckfords had inherited vast wealth, based on slavery and sugar in the West Indies, from William's father – Alderman Beckford of Blandford and the City of London. Through him came a connection with William Pitt, the Prime Minister. [The Pitt family had long connections with Blandford: all descended from Apothecary Pitt of Blandford (c. 1545), Governor Pitt of Blandford St. Mary (1653 – 1726), and Christopher Pitt, the rector of Pimperne (1699 – 1748)]. In 1756, during the Seven Years' War, when the nation was engaged in a fierce struggle for colonial supremacy in North America against France, General Wolfe, in planning his campaign in Canada, turned for help to his friend Alderman Beckford, who was able to influence the Prime Minister. As a result, General Wolfe took his troops down to Shroton, and the slopes of Hambledon Hill in particular, for training.

> *In the beginning of August 1756 a camp was formed at Shroton, near Blandford, in Dorsetshire, whence Wolfe writes on the 4th, saying that six battalions of infantry, six squadrons and two troops of light horse, with twelve pieces of artillery, were encamped upon a pleasant dry spot open to the wind, which scoured the camp and purified it. They had plenty of wood, straw, bread and meat, and good care was*

---

[42] *Dorset.* Michael Pitt-Rivers. p. 124.

taken of the men. This sort of life agreed well with himself, and his health was much better in the open air. His new colonel looked into and ordered everything for the best; and the vigilance of the commanders of the respective corps was to be praised.[43]

Thus, by an extraordinary coincidence, the significance of which was not lost upon Richard, it may have been that the troops which ascended the Heights of Abraham in 1759 and captured Quebec, thus ensuring that Canada would become part of the British Empire, were trained in Dorset. To this day the council houses built alongside the fairfield and the cricket pitch at Shroton are called 'General Wolfe Close' – a title secured to Richard's great delight when, for many years, he represented Shroton on the Blandford Rural District Council.

....

....

In the spring of 1946 these romantic associations were not yet understood or appreciated. The family was establishing a routine of separation from home during term-time that was to be the pattern of our lives for the next few years. Richard was serving with the RAF in northern Germany attached to BAOR (British Army of Occupation in the Rhineland). Margaret was trying to create a home out of the ruin that was the rectory at that time. Bess, Pat and I were away at boarding school, while Mary went across the road to the village school, leaving Gillian, not yet three years old, at home. A letter I received from my father during the spring term, when I was preparing for the scholarship examination to Sherborne School, sets the scene well:

BSRU, ROYAL AIR FORCE,

BAFO, BAOR.

MARCH 1946
    MY DEAR BILL,

---

[43] *Life of Major-General James Wolfe.* Robert Wright. p. 347.

THIS FUNNY TYPEWRITER WHICH HAS BEEN
ALLOTED TO ME IS ONE WHICH IS NORMALLY USED IN THE RAF
FOR TYPING OUT SIGNALS AND TELEGRAMS WHICH IS WHY IT
ONLY HAS CAPITALS. IT IS THE ONLY MACHINE AVAILABLE SO
I MUST MAKE THE BEST USE OF IT.

I HOPE YOU GOT BACK TO SCHOOL QUITE SAFELY. I AM
GLAD THAT I WAS ABLE TO COME HOME FOR A FEW DAYS TO SEE
YOU ALL BEFORE YOU WENT BACK. HOWEVER, WE CAN LOOK
FORWARD TO SPENDING THE SUMMER HOLIDAYS TOGETHER
SOMEWHERE. PERHAPS I SHALL BE ABLE TO BUY A TENT AND WE
COULD HAVE A CAMPING HOLIDAY.

SPRING IS LATE IN GERMANY BUT I WAS PLEASED TO
FIND THE LEAVES AND BLOSSOM ON THE TREES WHEN I
RETURNED. EVERYTHING LOOKS MORE CHEERFUL AND HAPPY.

I AM LOOKING FORWARD TO BEING ABLE TO DRIVE YOU
TO SHERBORNE FOR THE EXAMINATION. DO NOT WORRY ABOUT IT,
JUST DO YOUR BEST AND AS MUCH WORK AS YOU CAN UNTIL
THEN. WE SHALL BE PROUD OF YOU IF YOU DO PASS, BUT
WHETHER YOU DO OR NOT MAKES NO DIFFERENCE TO OUR LOVE
FOR YOU. WE ARE ONLY ANXIOUS THAT YOU SHALL HAVE THE
BEST PREPARATION FOR LIFE POSSIBLE.

I SPEND NEXT WEEK AT A R.A.F. CHAPLAINS'
CONFERENCE IN HAMBURG. THE CHAPLAIN IN CHIEF WILL BE
THERE. AT THE CONCLUSION OF THE CONFERENCE HE WILL
RETURN TO THIS AIRFIELD WITH ME TO DEDICATE MY NEW
CHAPEL OF ST. AUGUSTINE.

I EXPECT IT FEELS VERY QUIET AT SHROTON RECTORY
NOW THAT WE HAVE ALL (OR NEARLY ALL) RETURNED TO SCHOOL.
PERHAPS THE BUILDERS WILL HAVE FINISHED ALL THEIR WORK
SOON. IT WILL BE NICE TO HAVE A PROPER BATH-TUB IN THE
HOUSE AGAIN.

ALL MY LOVE TO YOU. DADDY.

Even though there was no 'proper bath-tub' in the rectory it
is typical of Richard's sense of priorities that he was concerned to
have a 'proper chapel' on his RAF station in Germany. A few
months later he returned to England to receive his medical
discharge from the RAF Hospital at Halton. Once again defiant of
all authority to the last, his papers note that he refused all
inoculations and vaccinations.

The Shroton to which he returned that summer of 1946 was
still a vibrant rural community, though little of that survives now.
At its centre lay the church and all that it stood for; this Richard set
out to prove with all the energy and enthusiasm at his command.
The parish church, situated on the lower slope of Hambledon Hill

at the southern end of the village across the road from the rectory, was completely restored over the next few years. To help towards the cost of renewing its roof Richard and his Parochial Church Council decided to sell, much to the chagrin and displeasure of the diocesan authorities, two redundant 17th century silver flagons so valuable they were never removed from the bank. In addition the organ was removed from its inappropriate position where it filled the side chapel to the north of the choir. Its ancient wooden blower had to be charged laboriously by a hand-pump. This was a task I shared, when I was at home, with the village lads. They whiled away tedious sermons by carving their initials on the organ casing, something, as the rector's son, I dared not do! A choir was formed. A confirmation photo, taken at that time, shows Richard with the bishop and churchwarden, and a choir of no less than 23 individuals – not counting the bell-ringers, in whose company I was soon enrolled. Festivals were a real delight: the altar at Easter festooned with lilies from the greenhouses at Ranston and the whole church filled with produce at Harvest Festival. Christmas had a special magic all of its own, when it was my task to help set up the tree with its crib beneath. The whole church would be illuminated by candles, and an hour or so before the midnight service Richard would fill the place with smoke from incense. On New Year's Eve a muffled peal, maybe of Grandsire Doubles, would be rung. Then, after a brief prayer at midnight, a full peal would ring out, echoed, on clear crisp nights, from towers all the way up the valley towards Shaftesbury. The poet John Betjeman, who later became a close friend of Richard, has captured the spirit of such moments in his poem 'Dorset':

*Rime Instrinsica, Fontmell Magna, Sturminster Newton and
Melbury Bubb,
Whist upon whist upon whist upon whist drive, in Institute,
Legion and Social Club,
Horny hands that hold the aces which this morning held the
plough –
While Tranter Reuben, T.S. Eliot, H.G. Wells and Edith Sitwell
lie
in Mellstock Churchyard now.*

11 Shroton 1945 - 1952.

Lord's Day bells from Bingham's Melcombe, Iwerne Minster,
Shroton, Plush,
Down the grass between the beeches, mellow in the evening hush.
Gloved the hands that hold the hymn-book, which this morning
milked the cow –
While Tranter Reuben, Mary Borden, Brian Howard and Harold
Acton lie
in Mellstock Churchyard now.

Light's abode, celestial Salem! Lamps of evening, smelling strong,
Gleaming on the pitch-pine, waiting, almost empty evensong:
From the aisles each window smiles on grave and grass and yew-
tree bough –
While Tranter Reuben, Gordon Selfridge, Edna Best and Thomas
Hardy lie
In Melstock Churchyard now.

A staunch support in all this work was John Biddlecombe, Edith's son. After a quiet war with the Royal Army Pay Corps at Bournemouth he had, with Richard's encouragement, decided to seek ordination and was training for the ministry at the Theological College in Salisbury. He had a car, a Ford Prefect, and in this he would arrive at Shroton with fellow ordinands, some of whom had turned to the priesthood after horrific war experiences; one man in particular was still emaciated after years in a prisoner-of-war camp in the Far East.

There was, of course, a church school, run by two devoted ladies, Mrs Cousins and Miss Harvey. It was filled with children of all ages up to 11, when they moved on up to Shaftesbury. Naturally this was restored and renovated. [Sadly it has long since closed.] For older children there was a youth club, which used to meet in the rectory, until it moved out to a couple of the Nissen huts remaining on the lawn. These had been converted for use with a simple kitchen, meeting room and games room, equipped for ping-pong and billiards at which Bess and I became highly proficient. Richard became a leading light of the NABC (National Association of Boys' Clubs) and NAGCMC (National Association of Girls'

Clubs and Mixed Clubs) because in those years of the late 1940s and 1950s there was still no such thing as a 'pop' culture.

With a post-office, a pub and a village store, Harvey's, where fresh bread was baked every day, a farm-yard across the road where milk could be collected in a small churn, and an hourly bus-service through the village from Shaftesbury to Bournemouth via Blandford, Shroton was still a real community. But it was isolated and 'far from the madding crowd's ignoble strife': a trip to the cinema in Blandford, or even on special occasions to Bournemouth, was a significant treat. In summer the place seemed to go to sleep: I would sit on the kitchen step wondering what to do, watching an ancient village worthy cycling past so slowly that I thought he would fall off his bike. The arrival of Shroton Fair (traditionally associated since the Middle Ages with the Feast of the Holy Cross on September 14th) marked the end of the summer holidays: it was a sign to get out the trunks, grapple with the dreaded clothing list and prepare for another school term.

The rectory became the focus of family life. It was an elegant late-Georgian structure with its main rooms facing east over the lawn and meadows by the river Iwerne. To the north was a large walled-garden, never used, while beyond were five acres of glebe land, now colonised by a host of suburban villas. Into this home Richard and Margaret poured all their energies, he in creating a learned country clergyman's residence, she in presiding over endless meals and ready always to respond to the call: "Is it time for a cup of tea Margaret?" But their first task was to make the house habitable. That first winter of 1945/6 there was no bath, nor was there much heating or hot water. It was never a warm house in winter: we would huddle for comfort around the large log fire in the drawing-room and it was my job to keep the log baskets well stocked with fuel. The girls shared the washing-up for which, at the beginning of the holidays, Bess would produce a rota. [A footnote was added 'Bill is expected to help out occasionally']. Margaret had a loyal helper in Mrs Galpin from the village who came in every day and grappled with enormous piles of laundry, out in the wash-room beyond the kitchen. It was some time before we had a fridge. But in summer the house came into its own. It was deliciously cool, with morning sunshine pouring into the three elegant reception rooms overlooking the lawn and its magnificent beech tree. Richard's study at the south-eastern corner, with its book-lined walls, clocks, furniture and Adrian Dingle's portrait of himself over the fireplace, became the centre of his life. My own study-bedroom on the floor above was the only room facing south; from its window I could take pot-shots at squirrels in the chestnut tree beyond the tennis court. I was given a fine desk over which I grappled, later on, with the mysteries of New Testament Greek [I still use it to this day]. Our parents and my sisters occupied the bedrooms facing east, and up in the attic was another warren of rooms, originally for servants, which were, in due course, converted for use by members of the family.

It was some years before the house was fully reconstructed. Immediately after the war it was almost impossible to obtain building supplies and Richard seemed to wage an endless battle with the Diocesan 'Dilapidations Board' about funding for the process. But eventually the concrete foundations of the nissen huts were removed from the lawn and a grass tennis-court was laid out. A swing was suspended from a lower branch of the beech tree, much used by the girls, especially immediately after meals. We even had a croquet lawn. (On one occasion I nearly killed old Mrs Biddlecombe, when a wild swipe at a croquet ball sent it whizzing over the lawn at head-height just by her ear).

....

In September 1946 I went off to public school at Sherborne some 20 miles away. It was close enough to be able to come home for the occasional Saturday afternoon exeat: I even cycled over on one or two occasions. But, for the most part, we children were not expected to come home during term-time and certainly there was no half-term break. Consequently Shroton Rectory and all that it stood for held a certain bitter-sweet quality in our memories and imaginations, forever associated with holidays. Only for Gillian, and in due course, our young brother John, was it ever a permanent home. [My own memories of public-school life are not an essential part of this narrative: I shall try – sometimes not too hard – to avoid them intruding into the larger story of family life].

THE RIVER GOES ON

1947 was an eventful year. It began with a bitterly cold winter after Christmas when the lake at Sherborne Castle was frozen. Life for everyone was miserable with the whole nation still trying to recover from the effects of the war. There was a shortage of almost everything, especially fuel. (The fields below William's house at North Wingfield were dug up to extract the coal beneath, the slag heaps of the coal mines all around the village blazing at night.) Margaret's sister, Kathleen, with her husband, Archie Symes, came over on a visit from Saskatchewan, where the temperature at that time of the year was regularly many degrees below zero. "I've never been so cold in my life!" muttered Archie as he shivered by the fire in the dining-room. (I suspect his father, Canon Symes of Parkstone, had just died, because Richard inherited his large theological library and the book-shelves that lined the west wall of his study). I was allowed home for my 14th birthday on the 20th March: it was a blessed escape from all the terrors of life at School House. I returned to school that day clutching a precious copy of Arthur Mee's 'Book of Everlasting Things' in my hand: it was an anthology of inspirational literature and prose, which I still possess. With great delight I read it by the pot-bellied coke stove in the day-room around which we gathered for warmth. On one occasion that term the actor Bernard Miles popped in and quizzed us about life in a public school. He, with Richard Attenborough, was taking part in the Boulting brothers' film 'The Guinea Pig'. (At that time there was a government proposal called 'The Fleming Scheme' to try and introduce working-class boys to public school: it failed.)

The summer of 1947 by contrast was glorious. David Sheppard, (later Bishop of Liverpool), then in the VIth Form, made 104 not out for the 1st X1: the lanes around Shroton, when I came home for an exeat, were magical green tunnels filled with the delicate flowers of cow parsley, or 'Queen Anne's Lace' as it was called locally; Margaret, as a special treat, would provide a lunch of roast lamb, with mint sauce, new potatoes and broad beans – a meal that still evokes precious memories for my brother and me.

Then tragedy struck. On 27th May Richard's beloved mother, Elizabeth, died. The cause of her death was never revealed to me; I was just summoned to my headmaster's study and told

"Your grandmother is dead". Richard must have been devastated: he had always been close to his mother; she it was who had kept up his spirits with parcels of books during the lonely days at Prince Albert and Fort Pitt, before Margaret came on the scene. Now she was gone. To make matters worse, his father, William, then proceeded, almost immediately, to announce his engagement to Elizabeth Ainsworth of Hag Hill farm near Chesterfield, the recently widowed wife of one of his masonic friends. (A trained nurse, she once told me with pride how in childhood she had met Florence Nightingale, whose country home was in Derbyshire and who died at the age of 90 in 1910). There was nothing untoward in the relationship, but it was all so sudden.

It was indeed an extraordinary summer. Towards the end of term an epidemic of infantile paralysis (polio) broke out at Sherborne School in which at least one pupil died. Like other boys who lived locally I was allowed home early, much to the disgust of my housemaster, who couldn't understand why one should prefer the comforts of home life to the miseries of School House. Notwithstanding the fear of infection the Mottershaw family came down to stay with us; then we all went up to Derbyshire to meet the new Elizabeth. In September her marriage to Daddy Doe took place at Shroton when Richard officiated. But we children were not there, except Gillian; even Mary had now started boarding-school before she was eight years' old.

After all this it is not surprising that early in 1948 Margaret became restless. Married now for 17 years, with five children to show for it, she had seen nothing of her own family during that time except for brief visits by her sisters, Mildred to the Manitoulin Island and Kathleen to Shroton. In addition her dear Father, Fred, had died in 1941. During the war brave souls such as Paul Gibbs, Dennis Taylor and Bill Blackstock had turned up to remind her of home. Now she wanted to renew her links with Canada, but many questions had to be answered. How was this to be done, when it was almost impossible to obtain passages across the Atlantic? How long should she stay? Who would pay for it? First of all a passport had to be obtained. (She must have travelled to England in 1936 on a joint passport with Richard, Bess and me). Then it was discovered that her birth had never been registered – not an easy task when one realises how far from any register office the settlement at Edam was. Eventually, with Daisy's help both the birth certificate and the passport were issued.

Richard had written to the Immigration Branch of the Canadian Department of Mines and Resources in London stating that he wished 'to go forward with his family to join his mother-in-law, Mrs G.F. Pepper, of Frenchman Butte, Saskatchewan, expecting that his wife will precede him'. Does this letter mean that Richard was getting fed up already with life at Shroton and imagined, for a moment, that he could make a fresh start in Canada again? Maybe he had begun to realise that, with his background and education, his future in the Church of England was likely to condemn him to remain a country parson in an obscure, but lovely, part of north Dorset! One can only imagine that long and anxious conversations took place beside the log fire in the drawing room of the rectory that spring [as Margaret sadly confirmed to us in her 93rd year]. Eventually it was agreed that immediately after Easter at the beginning of the summer term Margaret would go back to Canada on her own for a brief visit. With some difficulty a return passage was booked in the SS Ascania (the ship being otherwise full of G.I. brides) and off she went, with just a few pounds in her pocket, to spend a few weeks back in the bosom of her beloved Canadian family, who turned up in force to meet her at Saskatoon station, leaving Richard to manage on his own, looking after Gillian.

By the end of June she was back in Shroton again, ready to prepare for the summer holidays, all thoughts and dreams of a new life together in Saskatchewan forgotten forever. Indeed it is difficult to imagine how the family could have survived a move to Canada at that time. We children, with the help of Mrs Biddlecombe, were committed to an English boarding school education and Richard seems to have determined to make his own idiosyncratic way in the ministry of the Church of England. But we kept up a romantic image of life in North America fostered by assiduous reading of The Saturday Evening Post with its folksy cover pictures by Norman Rockwell.

In September 1948 Richard and I went on holiday together to Switzerland. The hand of Mrs Biddlecombe must have been behind this: she had spent some time in Switzerland as a young woman and ever indulgent to Richard she probably believed that he also ought to have a holiday abroad. In addition there was feeling that my father and I needed some time alone together. Vivid memories remain from that visit. We travelled by train from Victoria on the 'Golden Arrow' with but £25 between us, the maximum currency we were allowed to take abroad. After an exciting overnight journey through France, it was my first experience of mainland Europe, we stopped early next day at Basel. The refreshment kiosk there was a marvel to behold! It was laden with unlimited quantities of sweets and chocolates (articles still rationed in England): to this day the sight of a bar of Toblerone always evokes sweet memories of that moment. Our destination was Lucerne, a convenient base for expeditions up the mountains or into neighbouring Lichtenstein. Walking out by the lake one day I was horrified to observe sitting on a bench the familiar figure of my housemaster with his two colleagues: all three of them were 'bachelors', Messrs. Gourlay, Walford and May. It may well have been the only occasion when my father spoke to them. A more poignant encounter took place on the summit of either Mt. Rigi or Pilatus. Emerging from the carriage of the funicular railway we spotted ahead of us a group of young men in RAF uniform. What were they doing there? Quickly my dear father summed up the situation and holding my arm firmly, he whispered: "When they talk to you just behave naturally". Seconds later I understood what he meant. Glad to find someone with fellow experience of serving in the RAF (and maybe especially as a chaplain) they gathered around Richard. When they turned towards me I observed with horror that, without exception, their faces were terribly scarred and mutilated by burns. They had been trapped in the burning cockpits of aircraft during the war and now, for the moment, were guests of the Swiss government while undergoing lengthy treatment at the special burns unit at East Grinstead Hospital.

Returning to Shroton, to my astonishment, I found my closest school friend Christopher Penny installed in residence and busy making eyes at my lovely sister, Bess. He was one of the few day-boys at Sherborne and I used occasionally to escape to his home for a welcome high tea on Sunday afternoons. Brought up in

India, particularly in Kashmir, where his father was an official with the railway, Christopher was a natural athlete and physically well co-ordinated. Sadly his father had died suddenly while we were away in Switzerland, now he had been invited to stay with us for a while. It was difficult at first for us to use our Christian names when addressing each other! How jealous I was of his physical prowess! He could swim like a fish, walk about on his hands with his feet in the air, and leap off from the swing when it reached its highest point and ascend like a monkey into the upper branches of the copper beech tree. But Bess was much impressed, especially when on a subsequent visit, some years later, he brought another friend with him called Brian McMaster, the man who was to become her husband.

During the Easter holidays of 1949 I came down to breakfast one day to find my mother on her own in the kitchen. I can't remember what the girls were up to. "Mother", I said (as a young public-school lad I could no longer use the familiar term 'Mummy') "I had a strange dream last night. I dreamt that you were going to have a baby!" Maybe I had twigged from some innocent remark in conversation that she was pregnant. With a sweet blush she admitted that my dream was true. Some six or seven months later, when I was having lunch in the old mediaeval dining hall at School House, I received a telegram conveying the welcome and wonderful news that my brother John had arrived – on 17th November, as Richard proudly announced in the columns of the Times; "The gift of a son". Now our family was complete: all six of us - two boys and four girls, with sixteen years between my brother and me.

Holidays then were a mixture of fun and social ordeals. John Biddlecombe and I became godfathers to my little brother, towards whom for many years I felt more avuncular than fraternal. I used to take him for drives in the family car – another Ford Prefect – when I had passed my test. Once I came home from school and sat beaming with delight at the lad as he played with some tiddlywinks on the carpet. After a while I noticed that their numbers were decreasing. "Is it alright for John to eat them?" I exclaimed to Mother. A few days later they reappeared though somewhat faded in colour. Meanwhile Bess and I, and sometimes with Pat, were invited to 'young cocktails', when we stood around in fearful shyness drinking awful concoctions such as 'gin and orange'. It was an awful ordeal. I was measured for a dinner jacket at Hepworths in Blandford; we learnt to dance; Mother made party dresses for the girls; after Christmas a grand old lady who lived up at the other end of the village, Mrs Farquharson, would take us to a party at Eastbury House in Tarrant Gunville. At school the first long-playing records began to appear, brought over from the States by another friend – Andrew Waugh. [His father, Alec, having been struck off the Old Shirburnian Register years earlier for writing in 'The Loom of Youth', an exposé of public school life, had just been reinstated. Evelyn was his uncle].

Then in July 1951 I left school secure, I thought, in the knowledge that I had a place to read medicine in October at Jesus College, Cambridge. That this was not to be so, for financial reasons only, is not part of this story. Instead I decided to get on with my National Service in the Royal Navy. All of us, in one way or another, were about to go our separate ways and create our own narratives. On February 6th 1952 King George Vl died and with it we all hoped and believed that a new Elizabethan era was about to begin. Thus it was a quiet moment of triumph for Richard and Margaret when they were invited to attend the young Queen's first Garden Party at Buckingham Palace in July. It was a timely recognition for Richard and Margaret for all the good work that they had done in Canada.

In the summer of 1951 there was another moment of triumph and joy for them when it was agreed that Shroton should celebrate the Festival of Britain in its own particular way. (That summer the whole country, led by a Labour government, commemorated the centenary of the 1851 Great Exhibition). A pageant was produced to celebrate the complete restoration of the village school. This was the culmination of a heroic period of effort by Richard: in many ways it was another high point in his ministry. All his talents and love of history were poured into writing a narrative commemorating significant events in the life of the school and the village. This included the school's foundation in 1640, the battle against Cromwell's troops on Hambledon Hill, the Restoration of the monarchy in 1660, and the arrival of General

Wolfe with his troops to train for the campaign in Canada. An ancient descendant of Queen Victoria, Princess Marie Louise, was dug out from obscurity to preside over the occasion. She was escorted by that high Anglican, the Earl of Shaftesbury. The Bishop of Sherborne preached; soldiers from Blandford Camp donned 18th century uniforms. Ecclesiastical authorities such as archdeacons and the chairman of the Diocesan Board of Education turned up. The actress Patricia Laffan portrayed Queen Anne and men and women from the village took part in the pageant produced by an artistic friend of Richard, Peter Farquharson. Perhaps even more extraordinarily we children were allowed home from school in the middle of the summer term. So while Bess dressed up and took part in the show, Pat, Mary and I watched, while Gillian, no doubt, was among the children of the Lady Elizabeth Freke School. John, still a toddler, not yet two years old, participated in his own special way. "I remember Shroton's Pageant in 1951", said Gillian many years later, "and the Coronation that followed in 1953: how I went back to Croft House School [at Shillingstone nearby] after the bonfires were lit on Hambledon Hill".

....

....

Epilogue

'Lark Rise',
St. Neots.

St. Neots lies on the bank of the river Great Ouse where, to the west, the flat landscape of the Fens begins to slope upwards to the plateau that is Northamptonshire. In the middle of this countryside is the village of Little Gidding to which I was taken by my chaplain, Roland Walls, during my time at Corpus. In 1625 Nicholas Ferrar established an Anglican religious community at Little Gidding. It did not last long. Recent attempts to revive it have failed. But on at least three occasions in the early 17th century King Charles l came to visit it. In one of the darkest years of the Second World War, 1942 (the year that Richard joined the RAF), it was also visited by the poet T.S. Eliot, who found in it the inspiration for the last and finest of his 'Four Quartets': 'Little Gidding'.

I do not exaggerate when I say that it is words from Little Gidding which have provided the motivation for this attempt to tell the story of a family. 'In my beginning is my end' wrote T.S. Eliot and in the fall of 2002 as Lottie and I, with real 'fear and trembling', made our pilgrimage to Mindemoya and Fort Pitt, I could not help but recall his other words;

> *We shall not cease from exploration*
> *And the end of all our exploring*
> *Will be to arrive where we started*
> *And know the place for the first time.*

Before we went back to Canada I said to Margaret, my mother, then in her 91st year: "I intend to visit and give your love to all your surviving siblings". This we were able to do. Since my return I have completed this memoir and shared its final chapters with her as she sits, frail and confused, awaiting the end in a Wiltshire nursing home.

Attached to the wooden casing of the magnificent organ of Salisbury Cathedral are two lovely engraved glass panels by Laurence Whistler. They show the familiar lower slopes and outline of Hambledon Hill and Hod Hill as they can be seen from the valley of the river Stour: they frame these other words from 'Little Gidding':

And all shall be well and
All manner of things shall be well
When the tongues of flame are in-folded
Into the crowned knot of fire
And the fire and the rose are one.

We die with the dying:
See they depart, and we go with them.
The moment of the rose and the moment of the yew tree
Are of equal duration.

I am glad to use them as an epitaph and an expression of love and gratitude for all that Richard and Margaret gave to us.

Bill Taylor

St. Valentine's Day   14th February 2004

Bibliography

Grapes of Wrath. John Steinbeck. (Penguin 1951)

This is what happened. W.A. Taylor's memoir (abbreviated TIWH)

Canada. The foundations of its future. Stephen Leacock. (Montreal 1941)

Native Peoples and Cultures of Canada. Alan D. McMillan. (Vancouver 1988) abb. NPCC.

The Book of the West. H.A. Kennedy. (Toronto 1925)

The Palliser Expedition. Irene M. Spry. (Macmillan. Toronto 1963)

Fort Pitt History Unfolding. 1829 – 1985. (Fort Pitt Historical Society. 1985) abb. FPH.

The National Dream. Pierre Berton. (Penguin Canada 1989)

Landscapes and Memories. John Prebble. (Harper/Collins 1993)

The Doctor rode side-saddle. Ruth Matheson Buck. (McClelland and Stewart.Toronto 1974)

Sacred Places in North America. Courtney Milne. (Penguin Canada 1994)

Exploring Manitoulin. Shelley J. Pearen. (University of Toronto 1993)

Dorset: Tarrant to Blandford. Rena Gardiner. (Workshop Press, Blandford 1970)

England's Thousand Best Churches. Simon Jenkins. (Penguin 2000)

William Temple. F.A. Iremonger. (Oxford University Press 1948)

The Second World War. John Keegan. (Arrow 1990)

Hambledon Hill. A Neolithic Landscape. Roger Mercer. (Edinburgh University Press 1980)

Oxford History of Roman Britain. Peter Salway. (Oxford University Press 1993)

Pagans and Christians. Robin Lane Fox. (Viking 1986)

The King's War. 1641 – 47. C.V. Wedgwood. (Fontana 1966)

Life of Major-General James Wolfe. Robert Wright. (1864)

Dorset. Michael Pitt-Rivers. (Faber and Faber 1966)

Four Quartets. T.S. Eliot. (Faber and Faber 1959)

....

....